How to Get Along with *Almost* Everybody

Other books by Dr. Ray Guarendi
from EWTN Publishing:

Raising Upright Kids in an Upside-Down World: Defying the Anti-Parent Culture

Jesus, the Master Psychologist: Listen to Him

Thinking Like Jesus: The Psychology of a Faithful Disciple

Adoption: Should You, Could You, and Then What? Straight Answers from a Psychologist and Adoptive Father of Ten

Living Calm: Mastering Anger and Frustration

Taught by Ten: A Psychologist Father Learns from His Ten Children

Simple Steps to a Stronger Marriage

Standing Strong: Good Discipline Makes Great Teens

Family Faith Under Fire: Practical Answers to Everyday Challenges

Dr. Ray Guarendi

How to Get Along with *Almost* Everybody

EWTN Publishing, Inc.
Irondale, Alabama

Cover design by Emma Helstrom.

On the cover: two friends meeting each other (2236970225) and profile of a man (2176991217), images derived from Ljupco Smokovski / Shutterstock.com.

EWTN Publishing, Inc.
5817 Old Leeds Road, Irondale, AL 35210

Distributed by Sophia Institute Press, Box 5284, Manchester, NH 03108.

print ISBN 978-1-68278-391-7

ebook ISBN 978-1-68278-392-4

Library of Congress Control Number: 2024948842

First printing

Contents

Introduction 3
Why Try? 5
Watch Your Language. 13
What Is Difficult? 21
The More You Know 27
Show Some Interest. 31
Find Some Good Words 37
Misreading Motives 43
Going Easy 49
Unoffendability 53
Expectations versus Reality 59
The Urge to Surge 63
Agreeing to Argue 69

Overcorrecting 75
Instructive, Constructive, Destructive 83
The Off-Putters 91
Welcome Insults? 97
Snark Remarks 101
Petty Peeves 105
Just Ignore It 111
Speak Up or Shut Up 119
Damage Control 125
To Forgive 133
Time Limited 139
Almost Everybody? 143
About the Author 149

How to Get Along with *Almost* Everybody

Introduction

Actions speak louder than words. So says the adage. Kindness, charity, forgiveness, morality—divine directions from the all-time bestseller for treating others well: the Bible. The better you get along with God, the better you'll get along with people.

Actions do speak louder than words. But words speak loudly too. They are the everyday staples in our give-and-take with others. Indeed, relationships rise or fall with the use or misuse of words.

How we think, how we talk, how we react can set a relationship's course. Some habits and practices forge a connection. Some fray, even rupture it. Knowing which does what and when is core to getting along better with others.

Why Try?

To get along better with everybody—well, almost everybody—the first question to answer is "Why?" After all, are there any people in your life who just don't seem all that willing to get along better with you? What's more, do they seem okay with that? As they see it, you're the problem. They'd be easier to get along with if you were.

How much more of your time and effort is worth expending for little or no return? The temptation nags: Seek relief. Retreat from the relationship. Shun it if you can. But are these your only options? Or your best? Or even possible?

For most of us, the good relationships far outnumber the bad. Naturally so, as we gravitate toward those we find likable. You can choose those associations. Still, should your good to bad number twenty to one—a stellar ratio—one bad alone can commandeer your mind and mood, compelling you to waste emotional energy pondering the past and fretting the future. Not a pleasant state to revisit.

For those embracing the name Christian, the why is clear. More than that, it is obligatory. Jesus, the God-Man, the Master Psychologist, says so. Tolerance, forgiveness, kindness—all are at the heart of His teaching. They are not to be given only to those we think deserving but also to those we think much less so.

Jesus' command is a challenging one, and one He Himself lived to the utmost, even toward those plotting to kill Him. As far as I'm aware, no one is plotting to kill me or even smack me for trying to treat them better.

The Apostle Paul echoes Jesus: "If possible, as far as it depends upon you, live peaceable with all" (Rom. 12:18). St. Paul is not naïve about the human condition. He knows that not everyone will welcome our peace-seeking efforts. Nevertheless, he knows that most of us can do better.

One needn't be a Christian to want to be on good terms with others. Rare is the person who prefers chaos over calm, hostility over harmony, anger over amity. Humans are wired to seek accord.

Measured by the numbers, I think I'm doing pretty well with people. I have no conflicts with 99.999999-plus percent of the world's population. To my knowledge, not a soul in Europe, China, India, Africa, or nearly two hundred other countries thinks ill of me. To maintain my near-perfect record, I shun Twitter.

Closer to home, my numbers are still respectable. The mail carrier waves; I wave back. Meeting at the mailbox,

I ask, "How's your day?" She smiles, "Good. Yours too?" and hands me my mail. It's a cordial thirty seconds.

During games, my child's coach personifies Oscar the Grouch. Postgame, he's Mr. Rogers, speaking neighborly to me about my child's hustle, if not so much his skills. Whichever side of his persona I see when it's present for a season, maybe two, I can roll with the vacillations.

Most who crisscross our lives can be called temporary associates or friendly acquaintances. Our contacts are limited in number and time. Socializing with them is not all that demanding. Altogether, mine encourage me to think myself a fairly personable fellow. Again, by the numbers.

My family and inner social circle number much fewer. Yet they present far more occasions for me to act right or wrong, warm or cold, agreeable or disagreeable.

It's the law of social proximity: Those in my every day are also those who can most evoke not only my good but my bad. Do I treat them better or worse than I do friendly acquaintances? Am I less tolerant toward family than toward temporary associates? Do my family members see the petulant parts of me that few others do? Who gets more courtesy: those in my family or those outside? Am I lazy or sloppy interacting with those I claim to love most?

"Familiarity breeds contempt," claims the cynic. According to him, the more time spent around someone, the more you know him, and he you, warts and all. The natural outcome, if not contempt, is some degree of discord. Following his reasoning, about the only people we would like are those we don't know very well.

Real-life experience shows this to be nonsense. Our lives are shared with those we know, and still like, and truly love. Unlikable moments do not necessarily make for an unlikable relationship. Furthermore, we can lessen those moments should we want to do so. We are not bound by the cynic's prediction.

Honor thy father and mother—the fourth of God's commandments for a better life. What does "honor" mean? Do whatever they tell you? Yield to their every demand? Raise your children their way? No, no, and no. "Honor" means to grant them their due respect, as God Himself has granted them their role. It means to be very reluctant to sever your connection with them, and only for extreme reasons. That they are disagreeable or frustrating is not an extreme reason. Honor thy father and mother doesn't feature an asterisk that says: "Unless they are unpleasant or hard to endure."

You can choose your friends; you can't choose your parents. As a newborn, you couldn't browse a catalog of preferred profiles. As an adult, you can't mold them into your ideal. They are who they are, for better or worse. So, too, are your spouse's parents, if you're married, for better or worse. And your other family members, for better or worse. Getting along with those close to you can be up-close tough, but it also carries up-close rewards.

"Marriage is fifty-fifty. Each spouse gives equally." That may be the ideal. It's not the real. A good marriage is a blend of sixty-forty, seventy-thirty, or even ninety-ten, depending upon the issue. In most marital matters, one spouse or the other overlooks more, yields more, tolerates more. That's what makes a marriage work.

"It takes two to make a marriage work." What if the two are not equally working? What if one spouse is willing to work much harder? Can she alone improve the marriage or at least her side of it?

Not unusually, one spouse seeks counseling because of an unhappy marriage. The other refuses: "I'm doing just fine. I don't need that." Is she now defeated, forced to maritally tread water? Can she find some peace without her spouse's cooperation? Yes—she still has control over herself. Is she allowing unfair criticism to ruin her mood for hours or days? Does she take personally her spouse's acts of self-centeredness? Is she entangling herself in futile "I say, you say" arguments? In short, she can control her reactions so as to live more settled in an unsettled union.

Most divorces don't follow major dysfunction—abuse, alcoholism, adultery, mental disorders. Most divorces are the end point of a long-time interpersonal slide. Hurts and resentments have built upon themselves for years. "I don't like you anymore" sums up the marital state. As one old movie husband put it, "I don't like the way she licks postage stamps."

Our closest relationships—with spouse, parent, child, friend—have the most potential to test our limits to be calm, patient, and forgiving. Understandably so, as our emotions are wrapped tightly around those relationships. Yet they also have the most potential to shape our better nature, to make us better spouses, parents, and friends. Close connections carry the highest effort-to-reward ratio.

"I've tried everything. Nothing works," say discipline-defeated parents as they tell how they timed out, tuned out, and denied Buck every privilege except breathing. But along the way, they tried things that would have worked. They either didn't try them consistently enough or long enough. They mistakenly assumed that with just the right words, the right reasoning, the perfect discipline, Buck would surely be more cooperative by now. How long is this going to take?

Like disciplined-drained parents, relationship-rattled adults can surrender: "I've tried everything to get along with him. Nothing works." Again, what all has been tried? How consistently? For how long?

"I get anxious just thinking of being around her." "I find ways to avoid him at work." "A family get-together is no fun for me if she's there." "His religion put-downs are getting to me."

Interpersonal stress breeds personal distress. Frustration, anger, anxiety—all can linger long after a tough-to-take someone has left our presence. He's out of sight but not out of mind. The unpleasant encounter echoes in our heads. The question persists: Will he ever change?

Whether he will or won't, changing any relationship begins with the one person I can change—me. It begins with self-scrutiny: How can *I* be easier to live with? How can *I* be more agreeable? How can *I* be more likable? How can *I* be more patient with (insert name here)?

In self-help jargon, these are "how-tos." Every *how-to*, however, must be moved by a *want-to*. I must *want to* change. I must *will myself* to change. Absent the will, the best how-to will fail. It won't survive rebuffs or setbacks. Smoothing a rough-edged relationship can entail two steps forward, one step back. At times, two forward, two back.

The joke is: "How many psychologists does it take to change a light bulb? One, but the bulb has to really want to be changed." You can't change anyone without his cooperation. Changing yourself, however, may be the best way to get his cooperation. Put simply, changing you might just change another.

Watch Your Language

Language is a chameleon, a nimble one at that. It changes colors to match the latest hues of society's thinking. Words that not so long ago would have met with a "Huh?" are now used to color relationships. Most everyone knows what they mean, as they are spoken fluently.

Born in academia, raised in therapy, they've captured the cultural psyche. Psychologically, they sound heavy, alarming even.

Leading the new-speak are *toxic*, *narcissist*, and *emotional abuse*. The words declare the judgment: Some people are beyond social reach. Major defects mark their persona, making connecting with them, if not futile, emotionally exhausting. To safeguard one's well-being, therefore, calls for putting them at a distance or out of sight altogether. So dictates the language.

Extreme language saturates our everyday speech. Little Conan doesn't have a behavior problem; he has a behavior disorder. He isn't active; he's hyperactive. Big Conan doesn't have a temper; he has severe emotional dysregulation. The situation isn't bad; it is awful and terrible. It isn't good; it is amazing, beyond words. My chicken sandwich isn't tasty; it's awesome.

In case a word doesn't pack enough oomph, ever ready are universal prefixes: super, mega, major—as in super-awesome, mega-amazing, major terrible. We've no superlatives left to describe God. We've used them up on sandwiches.

Toxic—as in poisonous, as in deadly to one's health, not only physical health but also social and emotional.

Recalling a troubled history with her father, an individual is noticeably distressed. Listening intently, her therapist understands and empathizes. With more details, she asserts, "This sounds like a highly toxic relationship." Both ultimately agree that total father-daughter disengagement would be healthiest, at least until father becomes less toxic. Of course, with no contact, how is "less toxic" to be judged?

Before leaping from toxic to terminate, questions beg for answers. How accurate is daughter's portrayal of father? What is reality, and what is her perception? How would father describe the relationship? Can daughter do anything herself to reduce the "toxicity"? Does the estrangement include mother? How will other family members be affected? What might be the unintended fallout?

"My daughter and her husband upset me so much that I make excuses not to see them." "My mother-in-law is so critical that my spouse goes without me to her family gatherings." "My father is so disagreeable, I'm better off if I just avoid him." Suppose you poll twenty people who know your father. Sixteen of them concur that he is disagreeable and sour and that you would be right to sever ties. Suppose ten agree? Five? What number would justify crossing from "He's really hard to tolerate" to "I'm done with him"? The major factor: He is your father, not some acquaintance at church or a neighbor two houses down. Therefore, even a unanimous vote wouldn't confirm your decision. Yours is the only vote that counts.

In marriage counseling, two people give the history of their relationship. To say that both sound as though they live in separate homes would be a dramatic understatement. Both sound as though they live on separate planets. Their perspectives on the marriage and on who deserves more blame are worlds apart. Each thinking the other toxic is one perspective they do agree upon.

Generational rifts are now epidemic. More grown children want little or no contact with their parents, sometimes urged on by a counselor. What is so shun-worthy about Mom and Dad? Are they contemptible people? Are they so maladjusted that any kinship with them risks unendurable angst? Is the split the final outcome of long-term family dysfunction?

Often, no such picture is present. The parents are shun-worthy for one main reason: They are human, with all their imperfections—past and present. Should those imperfections be minor, no matter. In the children's minds, they are major. Disconnect is the answer.

Sadder still, many discarded parents raised their family in loving, faith-filled homes. Moving into young adulthood, the children came to believe, with the help of a God-abandoning culture, that their parents' religion is the very thing that makes them so unrelatable. Or, in a word, toxic.

Can a relationship legitimately be called toxic? Of course. It can be a serious threat to one's well-being—physically or personally. Still, "toxic" is the word du jour to characterize a whole range of relationships from the unpleasant to the very disturbed. Highly malleable, the word can also be stretched to cover people who don't deserve to be so called.

Someone might be, to me, a real headache. "Obnoxious" or "unpleasant" or "unlikable" doesn't quite describe him. I need a word with more punch. How about "toxic"?

It is said: Beauty is in the eye of the beholder. So, too, is toxic.

Narcissistic personality disorder—a diagnosis for someone so excessively self-absorbed as to be unable (unwilling?) to sustain close relationships. His self-image is highly inflated. He craves attention but lacks empathy for others. His "I'm always right" demeanor belies a fragile ego that is hypersensitive to any criticism.

The profile is an extreme one. It speaks to a severely stunted personality, making "narcissist" a narrow clinical term. Or so it once was. Nowadays, it's expanded to include those regarded as too much themselves and too little anybody else.

Further, a narcissist is consistent. He acts like a narcissist not with one or two people but with most. His persona permeates all his relationships.

An e-mail to me began: "I have been married for sixteen years, and about a month ago, I found out my husband is a narcissist. I came to this discovery while looking through articles and videos online for ways to understand him. How do I deal with a narcissistic husband?"

First, the Internet is not the most reliable place to diagnose someone. It can misinform as much as it informs.

Second, the marital discord has been long-standing. Discovering "narcissism" a month ago adds no new understanding to the marriage.

Third, the label marks husband as totally incapable of marital accord. He is driven by his pathology.

Finally, the reasoning is circular. Why is husband a narcissist? Because he acts the way he does. Why does he act that way? Because he's a narcissist. His conduct earns the label; the label is then used to explain his conduct. "Narcissist" sheds little light on causes or cures. It just provides a name.

To be sure, there are those who are "me first, you second," 20 percent give and 80 percent take. To call them narcissists, however, is to deposit them at the far end of abnormal. Call it my inner psychologist, but, to me, "narcissist" sounds much more impaired than self-centered. Most of us would admit to some self-centeredness. Few of us would admit to being a narcissist.

A grown daughter had not talked to her mother for four years, describing a turbulence stretching back into her teen years. Desperate to uncover some explanation for her mother's ways, she headed into the Internet—warning!—and, sure enough, "found a description of my mother—narcissism." A self-anointed "narcissist specialist" intoned that the only way to live with a narcissist is not to live with one; that is, to break the connection. So, following the one-size-fits-all prescription, daughter disowned her mother, who had reached out to her multiple times over the years. Recently becoming a Christian, she wondered how far "Honor thy mother" reaches. Furthermore, she spoke of years-long regrets, after disowning her mother at the urging of a label.

Whether disorder or description, narcissism is not a clear-cut malady that one either has or doesn't. It's a judgment call. And the one most often making the call is the one experiencing another's "narcissism." And that can certainly bias the judgment.

Emotional abuse. "Abuse" is a frightening word. On the spectrum of maltreatment, it resides on the extreme end. It speaks of an ugly, often traumatic experience.

Once preceded by "physical" or "sexual," "abuse" now includes harsh words and emotions.

Someone can insult, criticize, or mock me, meaning to hurt me. How much he succeeds is up to me. I may have little or no control over his nastiness, but I do have control over how hard it lands.

It isn't automatic: He acts bad; therefore, I get mad or sad. To emotionally "abuse" me, he needs my permission.

How much I feel mistreated lies more within my power than his (training in that power coming in pages ahead).

"Toxic," "narcissist," "emotional abuse"—all share a common feature. They have the potential to convince one to push another out of his life. They are shun words.

Who would I be more likely to write off: someone I think toxic or someone I think a terrific pain in the neck—or some lower anatomical part? Someone I see as a narcissist or someone I see as self-centered? Someone who abuses my emotions or someone who agitates them?

Short of a total shunning, these terms can persuade me that a relationship is so badly flawed that I'm wasting my time and effort trying to improve it. They can keep me focused on the other's personal deficits while ignoring any of my own.

Is all this playing word games? Whatever the language, the reality is the same. This person disturbs my peace. She provokes me to react to her in kind (in unkind?). Granted, but language does influence perspective. It can mark a relationship as hard to tolerate or as intolerable.

We act how we think. And how we think is shaped by the words we use.

What Is Difficult?

In a classic study, psychologists asked college students to complete a brand-new, state-of-the-art personality questionnaire. College sophomores and rats rank high among psychologists' favorite research subjects.

After reviewing their profiles, the students were asked: How well does this profile fit you? The consensus: Very well. The catch: All received the same profile. Those rascally psychologists.

Given the real range of student personalities, how did most of them report "Accurate"?

First, the profile was generic by design. It was filled with sweeping statements such as "While you can be outgoing, you do value your private times." "An unfamiliar social situation can make you feel a little uncomfortable, but after a while you adjust and enjoy yourself."

The psychologists gave their one-size-fits-all summary a name: Aunt Fanny. Meaning, it could describe anyone's hypothetical Aunt Fanny. In other words, a typical person.

Second, personality traits are broad summary statements open to individual interpretation.

"Truman is an honest person." What exactly does that mean? He won't tell the smallest lie; he'd never cheat a penny on his tax return; he gives his employer 100 percent; his word is his bond; he always says what he thinks. "Honest" could mean any one of these or more. It is particular behaviors that define the trait.

Bliss's mother is convinced that Bliss is strong-willed. Meeting with Mrs. Gradehard, her teacher, Mom hears, "Bliss is a delight in class. Never any problem. She's always eager to cooperate." Dumbstruck, Mom scrolls up a picture on her phone. "Is this the child? What school is this? Who are you?"

Is Bliss strong-willed or not? With Mom, she looks so. With teacher, not at all. Strong-willed, or its counterpart, "difficult," may be more or less apt given the setting. It's not who Bliss is wherever she is and whomever she's with.

A shy child at school may be rude and argumentative with Dad. An abrasive office worker may be regarded as a "saint" at her church. At the army base, the captain orders everyone around. At home, his five-year-old orders him around.

Are such inconsistencies signs of an erratic personality, or, as it's popularly called, a Jekyll-Hyde personality? Most often not. They are normal fluctuations depending upon time and place. A trait may sound like a consistent pattern, but it can be inconsistent across circumstances.

"Difficult" is one such trait. It is a catch-all word for someone hard to like or tough to get along with. It covers a sundry set of off-putting behaviors. Ask several people, "What makes someone difficult for you?" and the answers will range: "He brags constantly." "She thinks she's always right." "His temper flares fast." "She is really moody." "He acts like he's superior to everyone else."

Like all traits, though, "difficult" doesn't characterize the whole person. It may seem so because it's what affects you personally. The braggart, however, may be a generous guy, willing to give of his time to others. The trip-switch temper fellow feels quick remorse and struggles to curb his impulses. The self-centered woman is a devoted mother of five. She can't be completely self-centered.

Taking a more open look at another may not make him any less irksome to you, but it may make you less irked by him.

"My future sister-in-law and I don't get along all that well. But she seems to like the rest of my family." Does anyone else find her difficult? If not, then the trouble lurks in the relationship between you and her. What exactly does she do toward you, and how exactly do you respond? It's tempting, as well as comforting, to conclude, "She's just that way," rather than, "She's just that way with me."

Why another is difficult with you may not be all that apparent. Your cousin remains grudge-driven by something that happened between you as teens. You don't know what, and she won't say what. Your adult daughter is inexplicably distant toward you and your other children.

She's pulled away from the family for who knows what reasons. Your co-worker seems jealous of you, but you have no idea why.

We view others through the lens of our own personality, as they do us. Your father-in-law is fun-loving, laughs, and is quick with a quip. Around him, you are fun-loving and laugh easily. "Easygoing" would be his word for you.

Your own father is contrary and quick with a snip. Around him, you are ill at ease, wary of what dispute might be lurking around the next sentence. "Uptight" is his word for you.

So, who is right? Actually, both are. Each sees how you react to him. Who you are, and when, is moved by whom you're with and what they're like.

"I never saw this demanding side of my spouse when we were dating. Is this who he really is, and I missed it? Or did he change?" Relationships routinely move through phases. "Difficult" may not be who someone is but who he is at a particular time with you or in his life. If things were once better, what made them so? More to the point, who made them so? It takes only one to rejuvenate better times.

A difficult person or a person who is difficult? Someone difficult with me but not so much with others? Someone more relatable once but less so now? Am I massaging words, or as a colleague called it, "wordsmithing"? Difficult is difficult, no matter how it's defined. Sort of. Influencing another to be more pleasant, however, begins with looking more closely at the when, where, and how he is difficult.

"He's just difficult" doesn't encourage seeking fixes. It encourages bare tolerance or a write-off.

"Difficult" is a word wide open to interpretation, depending upon who's using it. Just ask Aunt Fanny.

The More You Know

It seems that drivers are getting pricklier as they feel invisible behind a vehicle's windows. Not that long ago, the grace period to move on green could be several seconds before a horn scolded, "Go already!" Now, sitting for upwards of two seconds is asking for a blaring rebuke.

Recently, I sat immobile after a green light had commanded, "Move." For the record, I wasn't texting. My mind was meandering somewhere between how to lower the national debt and whether the designated hitter is good for baseball. A prolonged horn blast shattered my reverie. Properly chastened, I accelerated, but apparently not fast enough, as the fuming driver swung around me, his hand gesturing what looked to be "Goodbye."

My first thought was, "What's his problem?" My second thought was, "What really *is* his problem?" Is it just traffic-light impatience? Could anything else be driving him? An emergency? A big appointment? A rough day? A rough life? Did his angry horn signal an angry guy?

All this speculation from one traffic stop? My wife says I do overanalyze things. I'll have to think about that.

One light later, I felt myself softening toward this huffy driver. Was he still in a huff? If so, living so near the edge of ire has to be a rough road. I could drive away from him. He couldn't drive away from himself.

A video features a young man who, early one morning, comes across what looks to be an ordinary pair of sunglasses. Donning them, he soon finds they are anything but ordinary, as they reveal to him others' inner struggles. His restaurant server at breakfast botches his order. The glasses tell him: Earlier she was forced to leave her ill child with a neighbor. Upon the man's seeing a densely tattooed, disheveled teenager, the glasses reveal that she had to choose premature self-reliance over a chaotic home life. On appearances alone, the man's blind judgment would have been hasty and hard. Without the glasses, he wouldn't have been aware that the driver cutting him off was in a panicked rush to get his son to the emergency room. Instead, he would have bristled with "What's his problem?"

One doesn't need soul-searching sunglasses to know that most everyone walks through life with hidden hurts and struggles. It's often the explanation, though not always obvious, to "Why is he like this?"

A young mother told me about her childhood with a harsh and emotionally distant mother. Recently, she'd found out about her mother's own chaotic upbringing and lonely marriage. She was shocked. "Does knowing this ease your attitude toward your mother?" I asked. "Does it raise your tolerance? Are you now more willing to overlook her flaws?"

As said, a difficult person doesn't typically see himself as difficult or, for sure, as difficult as you see him. If he has an inkling, he's slow to admit it. As he sees it, his ways are understandable, given others' ways. Or, "It's not me; it's you."

"Difficult" has a companion: discontent. When one is difficult toward others, his own life reflects it. Interpersonal friction and personal serenity don't mesh well.

Do you know a difficult someone? Is she content? Positive? Easygoing? How quickly does she overreact to frustrations or when others don't act as she wishes? Put another way, does she trouble you, but even more so, does she trouble herself?

I once led a Bible study at a local jail. Few of the guys had an upbringing anywhere close to my own. What I was given, most weren't—two good parents, morals, discipline, opportunities. I'd heard the aphorism: "There but for the grace of God go I." Inside that jail, I saw it up close.

Could the guys' language be coarse? Of course. Could tempers erupt? Abruptly. Did some follow the code: Get what you can however? Followed. Still, as they talked about their family life—stretching the term—I heard how their yesterday reached into their today.

This is not to call bad good or right wrong. Or to accept a moral whatever. It is to recognize how a history can shape a personality. The more you know and understand another's past and present—who they are and why—the softer your judgement of that person. And softer judgment accompanies a better relationship.

Show Some Interest

The place: a preschool classroom. Your perch: a small chair built for preschoolers. Can you still squeeze into one of those? You're watching a gaggle of three- and four-year-olds skittering about mimicking random motion. Each is alighting on a chosen play station—sand, block, corn kernel, spray paint—just kidding. The teacher closed that one down last week.

Each station entertains two or more little ones until a bell rings for them to move to another. The younger children, for the most part, play solo, oblivious to any other child nearby. In developmental lingo, this is called parallel play. It's an early social stage.

The older children are more likely to play together. It's called cooperative play. Parallel play matures into cooperative play within a few years.

Something similar happens between grown-ups. Call it parallel talk.

PERSON 1. Our oldest is heading for college in the fall. That came fast. We're running ourselves ragged trying to weigh all her options.

PERSON 2. We went through the same thing with our first. We spent a lot less time on that with our second. We got better at knowing what was important and what wasn't.

PERSON 1. We're still weighing the pros and cons of each school, but what we think is a plus, our daughter thinks is a minus.

PERSON 2. Both of our kids were attracted to colleges that we weren't. We had plenty of arguments. Finally, we knew we had to make the call, no matter what they wanted.

PERSON 1. Our daughter seems to think you pick a college by the looks of its campus. Or what the dorm rooms look like.

PERSON 2. Our son wanted a place that allowed off-campus housing in the freshman year. While we were there, he asked a few kids what the party life was like.

PERSON 1. Our daughter isn't really into partying. She's more into her grades and test scores.

PERSON 2. Our son is really into his grades too. So I don't know why he asked about the partying. He graduated third in his class. We've been able to get some scholarship help.

Person 1 talks about person 1 and daughter. Person 2 talks about person 2 and son. The exchange travels along parallel tracks. There is little intersection. It follows the order: I'll talk me, then you talk you.

Let's change the order.

PERSON 1. Our oldest is heading for college in the fall. That came fast. We're running ourselves ragged trying to weigh all her options.

PERSON 2. That's got to be exhausting. What places are you looking at?

Person 1 tells where and why.

PERSON 2. Which ones are on your list so far?

Person 1 names two colleges.

PERSON 2. What makes them your top choices?

Person 1 speaks of location, cost, and the likelihood of scholarships.

PERSON 2. With your daughter's grades and high test scores, she should get some really good help. What kinds of things can you get these days?

Two very different conversations. The former is parallel; the latter is cooperative. It takes only one person to move from parallel to cooperative.

Have you ever met someone and immediately liked that person? Why the favorable first impression? Afterward you realized: She was interested in you. She wanted the bits and pieces of who you are, not to be nosy but to be genuinely attentive.

At around age seventeen, my son Jon asked, "Dad, how can I talk to a girl so she likes being around me?"

My wife, Randi, standing nearby, struggled to hide a look of "Let's see if Ray has learned anything since our first date."

"Jon, ask about her—her parents, family, school, sports. What does she like, dislike? Ask about her opinion on things. Talk more about her than you."

Being interested in another is a winsome style. It starts a relationship well. And it can restart a poor relationship.

Your "I do it better" brother-in-law can get really tiresome. His way is "the way," and yours is second-rate, if not dumb. "Why would you buy that make of car? That year, no less?" Your wife pleads, "Try to ignore his bragging. I know he can be annoying, but he is my brother."

Her brother is an avid landscaper. His place could grace the cover of *Better 'Scapes Today*. Your plastic plants die. Rather than defending your vehicle knowledge, explore his nursery knowledge. "How do you decide which plants to use?" "What makes them so healthy looking?" "What's the best layout?" "Where do you buy them?" "How did you get so interested in landscaping?"

At first, his eyebrow might rise skeptically. Why the sudden interest? You've never asked about all this before. Are you trying to dig up my defects? If you can persevere past his wariness, you might just plant a new idea: Sister's hubby is an okay guy.

Your mother believes your parenting could use some adjustment. She comments and corrects, and, each time, you listen less and argue more. Alter the dynamic. Start asking her about her own motherhood. I know, you've heard plenty without asking. You don't have to do anything she says; just listen and show interest. After she's past her initial shock, hearing your respect for her experience, she may show some for yours.

No one is without pursuits and passions. Almost all people, those easy to like and those not so, respond well to "Tell me about yourself." Genuine interest can pause the downward slide of a relationship. It could even reverse it.

Find Some Good Words

The second law of thermodynamics rules the universe. Also called the law of entropy, it states: Everything tends toward decay. Iron rusts, food rots (except processed snack food), mountains crumble, the sun will burn itself out one day. Fortunately, all of us should be long gone by then.

A parallel law can rule the universe of relationships. Call it the law of social entropy: The giving of good words—praise and compliments—decays. "She knows what I like about her, even if I don't say it much." "I appreciate what he does, but I could tell him more often, I guess." "I told her how great she looked on our wedding day. I don't need to repeat it." Compliment corrosion can affect any relationship, even a good one.

A whimsical comment on marriage says: During the first year, after each physical union, place a marble in a jar. Thereafter, with each union, remove a marble. Prediction: The jar will never be emptied. Exaggeration? Maybe.

Some couples might take two years to fill the jar and ten to empty it, if kids came fast. Nonetheless, the jar pictures truth. Early in a relationship, we try harder. We more readily see and say positives.

If once present, did the positives leave? Or did our noticing them leave? Recall the cynic's perspective: Familiarity breeds contempt. Such, he claims, is the course of relationships. The more you come to know another, the more you come to know his faults, which then eclipse his attributes.

Two answers to the cynic. One, faults don't negate attributes. Bad qualities don't cancel good qualities. They are separate and distinct features of every personality.

Two, familiarity also breeds admiration. The beauty of my wife's motherhood is not obvious until children arrive, nor her emotional strength until a crisis hits. Time doesn't expose only failings; it also exposes virtue.

Some decades back, a theory known as behaviorism burst onto the academic scene. It maintained: Behavior can mostly be explained by how one's environment reacts to it. Positive reactions—called reinforcers—strengthen behavior. Negative weaken or extinguish it. Among the more potent positive reinforcers are the social—praise and compliments.

While behaviorism ignores head input—how we interpret others' actions—it does emphasize the power of positives. Everyone—from the youngest preschooler to the oldest psychologist—responds well to elevating words.

For compliment-comatose marriages, I suggest an exercise: Make a list. Write down what you like, admire, and appreciate about your spouse. The list prompts each to re-identify qualities and talents each may have come to forget, neglect, or overlook.

My wife and I did something similar early in our marriage, before kids, when periods of privacy outside the bathroom were the norm. After sharing with Randi my lengthy list, I'd hand her what I composed about me and just ask her to sign it. Sometimes she did.

Why write? Why not say? Because putting thoughts to paper coaxes more to mind. Everyone has qualities, skills, and habits that are list-worthy. "You are patient with my mother. You listen when I talk. You're quick to say 'thank you.' You always ask how my day is going. You fix things as soon as they need fixing. Your hairstyle is flattering. You make a mean lasagna."

Phrasing is important. "You're less critical than you used to be. You listen a little longer before tuning me out. You're gaining less weight these days." (This one will get your list torched). "You're not as bad as you used to be." These are backhanded praises. They say more about the list-maker than the list-receiver.

The longer, the better. No catalogue of compliments is uplifting with only three entries. Its skimpiness is a slight. To use the cliché: It damns with faint praise.

A social observation: Our behavior is influenced not so much by what others think of us but by what we think they think of us. Tell me you think I'm a courteous person, and will I be more or less courteous around you? If I say, "You are so easygoing," will you try harder to live up to my impression? Would "You're patient with my mother" nudge you to be even more patient?

Strong relationships can still fall prey to the law of social entropy. Compliments are not so much consciously withheld as allowed to wane. Weak relationships fall prey to different dynamics. The bad suffocates the good. An accumulation of hurts, or resentments or ill-treatment, sets the overall tone, and with that comes less willingness to see any positives.

"I'd find some, if she had some." Exactly my point. No one is without positives. If it appears so, then two questions follow: One, is my perception so skewed that I see nothing worthwhile in another at all? And two, is this the only person in all my life devoid of attributes? However unpleasant or contrary, everyone has pieces of his personality and demeanor that aren't so.

Those in therapy often speak of a long and chaotic history of turbulent relationships. They've hurt, neglected, and mistreated others. Nevertheless, I listen for their strengths, some things good to build upon, not because I'm such an affirming type but because no one I've counseled is Lucifer.

Behavior psychologists use the term "successive approximation." It means to reward small, gradual steps toward a goal. It's the technique used to teach animals complex, human-like behavior. Think Shamu. We humans are immeasurably smarter than the smartest animals—well, maybe not Lassie—but the same principles can shape us too. To nudge someone to be nicer, don't wait until he's noticeably nicer. That day could be a ways off, if ever. Personal progress typically occurs by the inch, not the yard. Comment on any small sign. Use successive approximation. It works for Shamu.

"Complimenting him isn't easy. Too many bad experiences are in the way." In a relationship with more downs than ups, any ups seem long gone. The downs dominate, understandably, as they are emotionally reverberating. They come to characterize the relationship. Thus, finding a few ups takes a willful, deliberate effort. It doesn't happen naturally or easily.

Someone somewhere once observed, "Everything is about something else." Meaning, someone's real motives are not those apparent. A bit of overpsychologizing perhaps. Sometimes something is not about anything else. It is exactly what it appears—or sounds—to be.

Human nature is your ally. People want to believe that the good you say about them is true. They want to believe you believe it too. One compliment a month sounds foreign, out of place, insincere even. One a day is a second language.

"It would feel forced. It would sound forced." Pop psychology trumpets endlessly the "authentic self." That is, act as you feel. Don't act against your innermost desires.

What a blatant piece of psychological claptrap! How's that for sharing my authentic feelings? If followed closely, much that is good to say would go unsaid. Much that is good to do would go undone. Acting counter to one's feelings often is good, very good. I feel like sitting on the couch and eating chips rather than exercising. I'm itching to unload on my uncle for his ignorant religious slam instead of ignoring him. Living by one's authentic self can hurt a relationship as much as help it.

If there's an opening for a compliment, but you don't feel it, fake it. As long as your jaw isn't clenched, your teeth aren't gnashing, and your eyes aren't bulging, few people will notice that you're acting according to your inauthentic self. Speaking good words while lacking good feelings is far better than speaking no good words at all.

Whether the law of social entropy is ruling, or whether a relationship has deteriorated, good words are among the first casualties. Resurrecting even a few fosters a better relationship, or at least a less poor one.

Misreading Motives

What does good counseling do? It probes thinking—the sound and unsound emotions; the helpful and hurtful behavior; the good and bad motives; the obvious and the obscure.

Trickiest to probe are motives, even for veteran therapists, even after listening long. Motives are fluid, volatile, hidden. The real motive can be buried beneath layers of apparent motives.

Just when I'm feeling pretty sure that my therapeutic efforts have uncovered the why of someone's conduct, another why surfaces, one that either doctors my understanding or upends it altogether. Humbling.

In or out of therapy, reading motives is an uncertain exercise. Words can be heard, behavior observed, but motives lie beyond the reach of the senses, leaving them open to assumption, speculation, guesswork. Like me, you may feel pretty sure about your judgment until . . .

Too, motives are as much mixed as simple. "He does A because of B" may be true as far as it goes, but it misses C, D, and E. What appears the obvious reason for someone's behavior may be only one of a number of reasons, any of which can be masked to him and you.

Reading motives permeates social interactions. Where people are, judging motives is. Sometimes the read proves accurate; sometimes it doesn't. Nonetheless, we trust on-the-spot judgments, despite the possibility they could be quite wrong.

A study found that clinicians formed a diagnosis within the early minutes of the first contact. Later details that supported their diagnosis were given more weight. Those that didn't, less. Even among those who analyze psyches for a living, first impressions form fast and resist correction.

Early impressions are best left flexible, open to adjustment in light of later impressions. Reversing a quick judgment—"I was wrong in thinking that about her"—can restart a new relationship and change the course of one heading downhill.

Juries weigh intent when reaching a verdict. A deliberate offense courts a heavier sentence than does one lacking intent, though both may have led to similar outcomes.

Likewise, when we judge that someone has purposefully wronged us, our sentence is certain: guilty as charged. When we judge he acted from ignorance, weakness, or some personal struggle, we are slower to convict. Discerning intent, though, can be tough. The best answer may be a definitive "I don't know." At the least, it gives another the same benefit of the doubt we would want.

We psychologist types, for all that we tout "transparency," can be sly when designing our experiments. What we tell our subjects (for those of you non-psychologists, that means "people") our objective is may not actually be our objective. We're studying something other than what we say we're studying.

In one study, researchers told subjects the question was: Would mild facial disfigurements foster discrimination in a job interview? So fake "scars" were placed on each face. Just prior to the interview, however, the scars supposedly needed some "touch-up work." In fact, unbeknownst to the interviewers, the scars were removed.

Post interview, many reported perceived discrimination, with some claiming that the interviewers made subtle references to their face. Because the interviewees were vigilant for any discrimination or bias, they heard some, even though its "cause" was absent.

A parallel marks relationships. You're convinced that someone doesn't like you all that much. You're now sensitive to any signs that reinforce that. The mindset is, "She doesn't care for me," so if she says something that can be heard either as benign or as a subtle slam, the favored interpretation is subtle slam. In fact, it's not meant so, but the past pushes in that direction. It just adds another blemish, a scar, if you will, on the relationship.

Prematurely assuming ill intent is rooted in a universal instinct: self-preservation. We are innately wired to survive, to evade assaults on our well-being. These assaults come no longer from lions and tigers and bears—oh my—but more from lies and taunts and blame. Hypervigilance thus becomes a shield against threatening motives.

"He seems to enjoy needling me." "I think she wants to make me feel bad." "His look says, 'In your face!'" The prime motive is to annoy *me*, to frustrate *me*, to put *me* down. Counselor types give this a name: personalization.

"My grandson's birthday party was set for a Sunday. I received the invitation from my daughter-in-law in the mail the Friday before. It looks like she doesn't care if I'm there or not."

Is this the only explanation? Or even the likely one? Does daughter-in-law have a pattern of late planning? Is she frazzled by juggling family and job? Was the party date changed at the last minute? Were all invites sent out together? Was the mail delayed?

"I don't know, but I do know I'm not her favorite person. We have a shaky history." When the motive is unclear, it's tempting to jump right to personalizing, to interpret current conduct in light of the past's. Each situation, however, needs to be judged independently. History doesn't always establish the present motive. And letting it do so can keep a shaky history from healing.

"I was slammed and didn't even know it. What does that say about me?" Maybe not much.

Personalization acts to protect the self. No one wants to look naïve or oblivious or foolish. Less personalizing, though, shows a more solid self-image. It shows the self-confidence to just shrug. Sometimes a shrug is the most insightful response.

Suppose Grandma is right. Daughter-in-law invited her but really didn't want to. Her "slip up" was, in fact, a personal slight. Does this now justify personalizing? That depends. (Don't you just love psychologists?) Does daughter-in-law slight others, too? Is this her way, along with a "Who cares" attitude? If so, the snub says more about daughter-in-law than Grandma. Taking behavior personally is questionable if that's how someone treats others too.

It's a typical workday morning for me. Two colleagues are chatting in the hallway. I offer a cheery "Morning"; one colleague smiles back, and the other launches a look saying, "You're interrupting us." What's that about? What did I do to you? My simple "Morning" is rude?

In my office, I hunt for motives. Maybe she was deep in crisis—family, health, work. Maybe her friend was upset about something, and she was being supportive. Maybe the Muzak piped in overhead was annoying.

Each I soon discard. Neither looked distressed. They were laughing. And the Muzak was playing "What the world needs now is love, sweet love."

What else? Does she dislike me, and I'm too oblivious to notice? Have I done or said something recently to bother her?

I'm at a loss. Nevertheless, my first instinct was to take her face personally. "What is it about *me* that prompted her stare glare?" Whether the explanation lay with (a) me,

(b) her, (c) the situation, or (d) all of the above is unknown. Then too, maybe tomorrow she'll give me a cheery, "Good morning," oblivious to yesterday's reception. All my personalizing wasted.

"Harmony likes to push my buttons." "Angel seems to get a kick out of arguing with me." "Hector enjoys badgering me." So lament parents personalizing a child's exasperating conduct.

Most kids don't plot how to best distress their parents. Overall, their motives are pretty basic—"I felt like it." "I had the opportunity." "I thought for sure I could get away with it." Kids are moved to do what they want to do, and if a parent gets upset in the process, well, that's just a by-product.

A high-profile court hearing illustrates a case of extreme personalizing. Having committed an egregious crime, the accused was facing the death penalty. Outside the courthouse, a group was protesting that penalty. Exiting the building one day, the man smirked and flung an obscene gesture. That did it! Some seemed ready to rethink their protesting. The crime was heinous enough. There was no need to add to it with personal insults.

The counsel is not "Don't read motives." Even if you tried not to, you couldn't succeed. Searching for what moves others is an ingrained social drive. The counsel is "Be cautious when you do read motives. Realize you could be wrong—by a little or a lot." Take it from one who reads motives for a career: Relationships can severely, sometimes irreparably, be marred by imputing motives that don't exist.

Going Easy

She's agreeable. He has a laid-back way about him. She can be very accommodating.

Each is, in a word, easygoing. The trait sits high on the likability scale. Its flipside—demanding—sits near the bottom. Easygoing people attract; demanding people repel.

What is easygoing not? It is not living by a moral "whatever." It is not being emotionally bullied. It is not buckling to every demand. It is not "I don't care what you do because I don't care much about you."

Easygoing is flexibility in the everyday give-and-take of relationships. It is an easy agreeability in minor matters.

A friend invites you to meet her at her favorite restaurant, a place that is a one-star on your "Better Dining Experience." Accept or decline? Join your friend or pass unless she switches venue? Which is easygoing? Find an upside: The service there is slow, but the food is so bland you don't mind waiting. Easygoing is sociable.

Your father bee-lines toward the front seat whenever he's a passenger. So do you. Do you plead your case? "Dad, I'm really more comfortable in the front seat." Bargain? "Let me ride shotgun this time; you take it next time." Or, without a word, do you slip into the back seat? Easygoing is respectful.

"Mom, no television, please," requests your son when his four-year-old son, Nielson, is with you. You hawk-like monitor the screen, so you see no reason to forgo grandma-grandson TV cuddle time. Debate or defer? Argue or acquiesce? Easygoing is adaptable.

It's marital movie night. Your spouse's choice is *Playground Puppies*. Yours is *The Grizzly Growls*. Which animals will share your evening? You offer, "You pick," hoping your spouse says, "Whatever you like." Instead, she goes with the pups. Now what? Can you nod, along with a "Sounds good"? At the theater, comfort yourself by ordering the fifty-five-gallon drum of popcorn with extra butter. Easygoing is easy giving.

Relationships are loaded with daily opportunities to be more easygoing. Few demand major concessions or wholesale personality compromises. Rather, they are small surrenders in pursuit of a smoother relationship.

"Comfort zone" is a pop-psychology catchphrase. It means to stay in a settled emotional state where one feels in control of his circumstances. Remaining within one's comfort zone is psychologically safe. Venturing too far out risks distress or anxiety. So goes the theory.

The comfort zone of a follower of Jesus should be broad and open to expanding. Aunt Agatha spends all of her day isolated in her nursing-home room. Just thinking of visiting her is unsettling—frail residents, outbursts, confusion. To walk into Aunt Agatha's world would be a jittery psychological trek. "Easy" would be the last word to describe it. "Queasy" is more fitting. At that, does comfort zone dictate whether or not to visit Aunt Agatha? Easygoing says, "This may be hard, but it's doable."

My seat at the end of the church pew where I always sit has my name engraved on it, as I see it anyway. At Christmas, the church is jammed. The usher motions for me to slide further down the pew—he must be a first-timer. A couple with young children is looking longingly at my end spot. They have two toddlers, which translates into being forced to leave the pew every eight minutes. Do I yield but pout all the way through the homily? Or do I smile and scoot over? Easygoing is welcoming.

Easygoing isn't always easy doing. A first-time minor concession can feel major and forced. Acting counter to one's at-the-moment preference comes easier with practice, however. Easygoing becomes a style.

Easygoing carries unforeseen benefits. For me, as a longtime softball player and coach, finding a team sponsor was tougher than finding players. So when a teammate told me of a business owner who was interested, I jumped at the possibility. Since I didn't know him, the three of us set up an early-morning breakfast meeting. Walking into the restaurant, I saw my friend sitting alone in a booth. "Bill called this morning and said something came up last night, and he can't make it." My first thought was, "If it came up last night, why didn't he tell us then?" Good thing I kept that to myself and instead said, "Well, then, let's get some breakfast." At which, Bill, overhearing me from the next booth, joined us, smiling. My teammate was part of the game plan. Bill wanted to see my reaction to his supposed "no-show." Would it be irked or collected? He sponsored us for years. And he picked up breakfast too.

A radio-station manager invited me to speak at the station's fundraising event. As I sat beforehand at my book table, an unfamiliar woman approached, perused my titles, and asked, "If I choose three of these, would you give them to me for free?" Wearing my best poker face while wondering about her request, I simply said, "Yes." Whereupon, she took the books, thanked me, and walked away. After the event, I found out that she donated twenty-five thousand dollars to the station. Then I understood: If she was planning to give a lot, she wanted to see if I was willing to give a little.

Did either situation offend me? Did I feel set up? No. Both individuals were considering financial support, so they had the right to measure my flexibility.

"What's best for you?" "Sure, I can do that." "You choose." "Sounds good." "You make the call." "I'm open to that." A few simple lines to say, "I want to be easygoing about this."

Unoffendability

Unoffendability—a mark of an easygoing individual, one very hard to offend.

"Unoffendability" is a neologism—a made-up word. *Merriam-Webster* annually adds words that were once neologisms but have rapidly saturated everyday speech. Here's hoping "unoffendability" one day lands on its pages.

Until then, here's a definition: "Unoffendability" is the ability to take little or no offense when taking offense would be the ordinary reaction. Taking little or no offense? When most would? Who can live up to this definition? Where people are, chances for offense are. Nonetheless, the quality—call it a virtue—is well worth every effort it takes to practice. The harder you are to offend, the easier you will live with others, as well as with yourself.

Unoffendability has an antagonist—prickliness. The word captures well society's bent toward taking harrumphing umbrage. Young people seek "safe spaces" to retreat from hearing anything counter to their sense of things. Politicians chew their words into mush so as not to miff potential voters. Teens stand cyber-ready to retaliate against anyone posting anything tagged as unacceptable. A street code warns to guard how you look at whom, and for how long, lest you provoke.

More people these days are keeping a sharper lookout (hear-out) for being "dissed," short for "disrespected." The culture keeps coining words to reflect its ongoing and on-growing petulance.

Underlying all this peevishness is what Christians call "Original Sin"—the inward bent toward the self and its desires. To be offended is to expect or demand that I be recognized, accepted, understood, or honored. None of this is due me, however. It may be what I want, but it is not my entitlement. Should I believe it is, I can feel cheated. And from there, it's a short misstep to being offended.

You are infinitely valuable—not because you declare it so, as the self-esteem movement declares, but because the Creator of the universe declares it so. As such, your self-worth is rock solid. It can't be yanked down by another's words. Nor by your own words.

Were it possible to fully fathom your worth in God's eyes, you would be impervious to offense. This side of Heaven, that isn't possible. This side of Heaven, it is possible to be less offendable.

Not all "offenses" are unfair or insulting or mean-spirited. An offense may also happen to be true. Defensiveness—self-protection—may be my first instinct should my wife tell me I don't listen to her well—or something like that, anyway. Before believing myself unjustly accused, would I better ask: Is this true?

While the truth can hurt—sometimes more than a falsehood—it isn't offensive. If taken so, a closer self-look is called for. Honestly answering "Is it true?" can dramatically reduce, even eliminate the offensive of someone's words. Even if they meant to offend, the truth is not a good means to do so.

"Taking offense" and "feeling offense" don't say the same thing. Taking offense needs the head's cooperation. Taking offense is reflective. It involves thinking, interpreting another's action.

Feeling offense is reflexive. Someone acts offensively, and automatically I react emotionally. The feelings take priority. The mind isn't engaged to settle them, not at the moment, anyway. Without better thinking, the emotions rule.

"I can overlook one offense, but that's harder when it keeps happening." Everyone's belly for offense has its limit. Even so, the same rethinking that cushions one offense can cushion similar ones. As one character in an old football movie observed after a trick play, "Worked once, oughta work again."

Repeat offenses are neither novel nor creative. They tend to target the same subjects, same remarks, same scolds. Their frequency alone discredits them. They get old. They don't say or do anything that is surprising. More often, they reveal more about the offender than the offended.

As with repeat criticism, they shouldn't bother more; they should bother less.

"How dare you!"—an attitude provoking being offended. "How dare he criticize my parenting—he should look at his own!" "How dare she call me judgmental—I'm the least judgmental person I know." "How dare she put me down, behind my back, no less. I don't deserve that."

Whether you do or don't deserve it, it happened. Someone said it. What's more, she may believe you do deserve it. In short, she did dare.

"I may not be able to change what somebody thinks, but I don't have to like what he thinks." Dislike is separate from offense. I dislike when my children make poor decisions. Their decisions, though, don't affect me directly. To be offended, I must think, "They shouldn't be doing this to me." In fact, they are not doing anything to me. Likely, I'm not even on their minds when they act poorly. Unless perhaps, "What's Dad going to think?" Well, Dad won't like it, but it isn't offensive to me.

Only one person never deserved offense. Only one person never sinned against anyone. Whatever He said, however pointed, was legitimate. At that, some reacted fiercely, to the point of plotting His death. "How dare He say that about us?"

Jesus endured more slander and scorn in three years than I will in a lifetime. Am I more worthy of respect than He? Do I challenge, "How dare they say that about me!"

St. Paul exhorts, "Put on the whole armor of God" (Eph. 6:11). He was bracing the first Christians for persecutions, coming through word or violence.

Can words threaten me physically? Yes, but rarely do they. Can they threaten my emotional well-being? Yes, but unlike with a physical assault, I have to allow an emotional assault.

"Sticks and stones can bruise my bones, but words can never hurt me"—a ditty from my school days. It has grown-up wisdom.

"Words can hurt. They can bruise. They do put down." Yes, they can do this and more but not by themselves. They must be given meaning by me. Words must be weighed by their who, when, and why to offend, whether more or less.

Suppose my father-in-law mocks my career. He calls it financially foolish. Does he know what he's talking about? Does his know-it-all attitude arise from his own career insecurities? Does he swipe at others, not just me? How I hear him determines his offensive punch. He talks demeaningly; therefore, I must feel demeaned? The latter doesn't follow the former.

My teenage son sees me as the crustiest Neanderthal to stalk the parenting landscape. Must I be hurt by his image of me? Knowing I'm acting for his own good and knowing his youth doesn't yet understand that, can I be pleased? Actually, he is complaining that my standards are unlike the crowds'. No offense taken, son. Compliment taken instead.

St. James warns: Control your tongue. Small but mighty, it's like a rudder able to steer a large ship (James 3:4–5). His warning is meant for those who speak wrongly, not for those wrongly spoken to. He knows we can't control anyone else's tongue, only ours.

Jesus says, "If anyone slaps you on your right cheek, turn to him the other also" (Matt. 5:39). In Jesus' culture, a cheek slap was a stinging show of contempt, one that wordlessly conveyed, "You're worthless!" With a vivid image, Jesus is emphasizing, "Don't let someone wrongly put you down. Silently respond, 'You can't make me feel insulted.' " Godly counsel when feeling verbally slapped.

"I try not to offend others. I would think they'd do the same for me." The Golden Rule says: Do to others what you would have them do to you. It does not say: If you do right to others, they will do right to you.

Unoffendability: It's an ideal, one not easily reached. Stretch for it, though, and relationships—the easy and the not so—improve. Fortunately, being unoffended does not so much depend upon others being unoffensive. It depends more upon you. How you think, not how they act, sets the conditions for how easy or how hard you are to offend.

Expectations versus Reality

A gold definition of "frustration": the difference between the way we want things to be and the way they are. It is the distance between our expectations and reality.

The definition fits relationships well. Frustration is the way we want others to be and the way they are. A theme I hear repeatedly as a psychologist: "Tell me how to make someone be different."

Expecting others to act well—to be moral, fair, respectful—is understandable. Treat me well, as I treat you. You would agree that I do treat you well, wouldn't you?

I can *hope* that another will act right toward me. I can *want* it. I can *pray* for it. If I should *expect* it, however, I'll set myself up for frustration or distress or anger. Because what I expect may not happen. Because someone *should* treat me right doesn't mean she *will*.

Expect can morph into demand. I not only *want* good treatment; I *demand* it. After all, there are accepted social rules. I may accept them. Another may not.

Expectations set too high can rattle the most solid relationship. Your sister is among your three favorite people. She has always been pleasant, agreeable, nice to be around—until yesterday, when she voiced a subtle slam against your spouse, who happens to be your number-one favorite person.

"Where did that come from? That's not who my sister is." That may not be who she is consistently, but it was at that moment, during that conversation. Did you mishear her? Are you overreacting? Has she always held that opinion?

Strong relationships have their bumps and bruises, as spouses in half-century marriages will confirm. To expect all smooth, all the time, is to be shaken when a rough spot occurs. "Are we as close as I thought?"

The saintliest person is not yet in Heaven. Earth-bound, she still sins, as does everyone. Expect that reality, and occasional "sins" against you won't corrode your connection. The cynic will be proven wrong: Familiarity doesn't breed contempt.

A woman had a friend who abruptly began to pull away. What do you think is going on, I asked. "She said I said something that offended her. When I asked her what it was, she told me. I didn't mean it at all like she took it, but I still apologized." Did she accept that? "She seemed to, but our friendship hasn't been the same since."

Had her friend been silently stewing and storing up "offenses"? Her latest "misspeak" didn't kill the friendship, but it chilled it. Like "toxic," offense is in the ear of the beholder.

Did she speak counter to her friend's philosophy? That being, a true friend doesn't say anything not friend-like. If she does, she breaks the pact. Her friend's faulty expectations were set to take down the relationship.

Unlike your delightful sister, your other sister pushes the limits of your sibling bond. She's just lobbed at you snarky remark number seventy-two, not all in one day, but over the last year or so. But who's counting? Later you stew, "Why does she do this? What is her point? Why does she keep trying to upset me?"

Here's a thought do-over: "Why do I keep upsetting myself? This is my sister's way. Nothing that I haven't heard before." Why does snark number seventy-two still have the same or more bite as snark number ten or forty or sixty? Their repetition alone should reduce their credibility and, with that, their bite.

An elderly widowed relative had always been ruled by her unruly emotions. When I visited, her moods were predictably unpredictable.

Why did I continue to visit? Because she was lonely, and others had pulled back—and because her distress didn't stress me. I was aware it could erupt anytime during any visit. I knew to expect it.

If her emotions had roiled mine, my visits would have trickled to a token "Hello" phone call at Christmas. Despite her moodiness, her spirits rose as soon as I walked in. And she always covered her table with a buffet. Chocolate and cookies can make riding someone's ups and downs easier.

"My spouse is quick to find fault with me." How long have you been married? "Twenty-one years." How long has he been finding fault? "I'd say about twenty of those years." Does it bother you now as much as it did then? "Every bit. Sometimes more." Why so? "Because it builds up. He knows how I feel. I keep waiting for him to stop." Do you expect him to stop? "He hasn't so far." Could you stop expecting him to stop? When you get another criticism, can you think, "Nothing new to hear. Same old stuff. Whatever."

Wife's lowered expectations won't immediately lower husband's criticism frequency. But it will make her less vulnerable to those criticisms and, with that, less reactive. And that itself could move him toward finding less fault.

To lower your expectations is not "I'm giving up on you." It is not "I'll get used to mistreatment." It is not "I don't care what you say or do because I don't care about you."

It's worth repeating—*did you expect that?*—to adjust expectations is to adjust thinking. It is to realize what has been, what is, and what may continue to be. Closing the gap between expectations and reality lowers frustration. We can't always alter reality. We can always alter our expectations.

The Urge to Surge

Adolescence found me jumping feet first into playing pick-up basketball, a sport I stretched into four decades. I felt the end nearing when my head ordered my legs, "Run!"—and they refused: "Why? Make us!" Or, when the ten-foot-high rim seemed to be laughing at me from what looked to be twelve feet up.

While my ball-control skills over the years showed noticeable slippage, basketball did pass on to me a life skill: mouth control.

B-ball demands self-restraint. Otherwise, after several "fouls," a player must leave the game. With ten bodies jostling for position, bumping against each other, the action gets pretty frenetic.

When my adrenaline-charged zeal threatened to override court courtesy, I made an adept move: I hustled off court. Sitting on the sidelines gave my heated emotions time to cool, and in usually a minute or so, I was settled enough to return to the game. Had I stayed on court, a foul was likely seconds away.

My strategy worked: Leave the scene, ease the steam, reenter the scene. Whether on or off the court, letting inflamed emotions settle even a little will leave undone or unsaid what is best left undone or unsaid.

It's a predictable relationship: The closer words are to fevered emotions, the more likely they are to be harsh, hurtful, or hateful. Therefore, if you can will yourself silent for a short time, sometimes more seconds, the urge to surge will plummet. Physiology is your teammate.

During my teens, I also began to lift weights. Long-time lifters can often bench-press three-hundred-plus pounds. Conquering that much gravity is inconceivable to the first-day-in-the-gym lifter.

The emotional parallels the physical. Restraining the tongue (weight—four ounces) during the rush of emotions can feel heavier than bench-pressing two hundred pounds. In the gym and in life, repetition triumphs. The once unthinkable becomes the possible, which becomes the doable.

"Even if I let my emotions cool for an hour, I'd still feel the urge to vent." Yes, but would you vent as hotly? Forty-plus years of therapy (not mine) has convinced me that most people have more self-control, a.k.a. willpower, than they believe. "I can't" often is "I won't" or "I don't want to."

Telling yourself, "Don't say it!" when your emotions are screaming, "Say it!" can feel futile at first. Weight Training 101: Begin with a manageable weight. Mouth Training 101:

Begin with a manageable delay—say, five seconds. Count silently if you must. After some successes, increase your "wait" to ten seconds, then twenty. As in weightlifting, what was once heavy will become your warm-up weight. And if you still do speak, your words will be more controlled. Lowered volume is easier to hear.

Behavior psychologists talk about "negative reinforcement." Contrary to popular misconception, it is not punishment. It is the withdrawal of a negative consequence to reward a behavior. For example, "Connor, you may leave the corner as soon as you're quiet." The desired behavior is peace—pretty much every parent's desire. The negative reinforcement is no more corner. Another illustration: After two weeks of gym visits, you no longer feel soreness in muscles you didn't know you had. No more soreness is the negative reinforcement. It can keep you exercising.

The negatives of an unbridled mouth—upset, anger, ill will—don't follow a bridled mouth. Silence is thus rewarded.

Far more damage comes from the badly said than from the unsaid. The saying is: You never have to apologize for what you didn't say. Neither do you have to do damage control.

To warn yourself, "Stay quiet" at the instant staying quiet feels nearly unreachable might sound like telling a fire-breathing four-year-old, "Settle down." Or someone anxious, "Relax." Or someone depressed, "Cheer up."

The analogies don't fit, however. One, anxiety and depression don't crest briefly, then subside. They tend to be enduring. Two, you have a stronger emotional governor than does a preschooler. You do, don't you?

"I speak my mind." Your mind or your emotions? Inflamed emotions don't reliably reveal what's in one's mind. They don't so much clear the air as cloud it. The hotter the words, the cooler their reception. Will you hear, "Phew. That was intense. But I'm glad you said it. I need to know how you feel. And I can only know that when you're really mad." Your words may be on target, but they won't connect if another feels like a target.

"You find out what someone thinks when she's upset." As alcohol can loosen the tongue enough to make public what heretofore has been private, so too can smoking emotions. Or so the reasoning goes.

Have you ever confessed, "I'm sorry. I didn't mean that. My emotions got the better of me"? Did you hear, "Yes, you did mean it. Your feelings said it." Or did you hear, "I understand. I've done the same." The former is faulty thinking. The latter is fair-minded.

"Feelings speak truth" is a mindset that can burn a relationship. Sometimes feelings speak only surging adrenaline.

"I tell it like it is." Like it is, or like you think it is? Perception may not at all be what actually is. Furthermore, would you think the same tomorrow—or even one hour from now? Fiery feelings can warp one's sense of reality.

Before telling it like it is, ask: What is my purpose? To help? To hurt? To retaliate? What is said to give another a dose of reality may not always do so, particularly if it hasn't done so in the past.

Of course, not all feeling-speak is reactive. Sometimes it's premeditated. While the emotional surge has passed, the urge to "speak my piece" remains. Again, have you spoken your piece prior? How often? The law of diminishing returns intrudes: The more you repeat your piece, the less it's accepted.

Is this all to say: Never speak up, no matter when, or to whom, or about what? Coming from a therapist, that would be heresy. It is to caution: Speak less from unruly emotions. Delay. Give the emotions time to ease, even a little. You don't have to fill the gap with positives. Just fill it with silence. You will be rewarded. So will the other person. Negative reinforcement works.

Agreeing to Argue

We argue a lot. We argue over little things. We argue loud and mean.

"We" is a plural pronoun, meaning that at least two parties are participating—though not always equally. Should one cease—through silence, concession, or apology—the quarrel quiets quicker. It loses momentum without mutual refuting and rebutting.

Marriage mentors intone: Good marriages have "good" arguments. They reveal and resolve differences. Avoiding all arguments risks inviting smoldering resentments.

A good argument adheres to a few basic rules. One, it doesn't devolve from courtesy to cutting. Two, all get a fair hearing. Three, it doesn't spark side arguments. Unfortunately, as temperatures rise, staying within the rules becomes iffy. As one comedian quipped, "When an argument starts with, 'What did you mean by that?,' it doesn't usually end with, 'Oh, now I know what you meant by that.' "

Arguments, however "good," are still not most people's idea of a good time. They tend to slip toward the critical and the personal. As often as not, they end up bruising more than bandaging, marring more than mending.

Disputes move in several directions. "I'm right about this—you're not." "I'm not guilty, and I have every right to defend myself." "I'm the reasonable one here." "Most people would see it my way."

When one is traveling an interstate highway, a construction zone can stall progress. Arguments travel likewise. They speed along until they hit a roadblock, and then no one budges. All that's left moving is frustration.

To avoid a traffic tangle, seek a nearby exit. To avoid a turbulent tangle, seek a nearby exit.

"Just listen" is one nearby exit. Perhaps it's a coincidence, or some farsighted linguist planned it so, but *listen* and *silent* contain the same letters. Though anagrams, their relationship is one-directional. You can be silent and not listen. But you can't listen if you're not silent.

Listening is a passive response. It requires no forming of counterarguments. It requires only attention, though it can demand self-restraint not to instantly react to what one is hearing.

In a therapy session, I may listen for much of the hour. "Maybe so, but you're getting paid to listen." Admitted, but that's not my motive. Before I talk, I must listen. If I speak too soon, my words could be futile or, worse, misguided.

To increase your listening stamina, prepare yourself. You may not at all like what you hear. But if you've heard it before, the shock is less. Expect it and you can listen longer.

What's a decent listen time? Half an hour? Ten minutes? Assuming you're not a therapist, how about one minute? Whatever negatives fill that minute, don't respond. Look at the speaker, not the ceiling, not the floor, and definitely not your watch. Don't yawn, eye-roll, or stare at the TV, especially if it's off.

Mr. Spock—the ultrarational, half-human, half-Vulcan from the original *Star Trek* television series—could calculate time to the fraction of a second. If you're not half-Vulcan, you may have to estimate one minute, as well as struggle to remain rational. Again, citing Einstein—"Time is relative"—a minute rushes by when packed with accolades. It crawls when not.

Any disinterest, dismissiveness, or disdain can undercut listening. The more so, it can rile. It tacitly declares: "I'm not really here; I'm just tolerating this."

"Are you even listening to me?" An ironic question. Just when you are truly trying to listen, you get accused of not doing so. "I am listening. I want to hear what you have to say," may both surprise and soothe. A change from the past can meet with "What is this?"

Listening is like tapping the brakes on a speeding dispute. It is like exiting the highway fifty yards before a construction tie-up. It dodges collisions.

Routinely in counseling, someone speaks to me of seething emotions, self-destructive choices, or hurting others. Were I to fire off "What are you thinking?" or "How can you even talk like this?" or "You really need to get yourself together," if he didn't abruptly walk out, he'd likely stop talking.

To hear what someone is thinking, in or out of therapy, listening before correcting is a first step to understanding. The second is to ask questions, seek specifics, clarify motives. In short, it is to venture inside another's head.

A wife speaks of a long-time marital sore spot. "He won't defend me when his mother criticizes me about anything—the kids, the house, my schedule." I ask her husband: Do you know why your wife thinks this? "Not really." Have you asked her? "Not really." Why is that? "Because I don't agree."

To understand does not mean to agree. What you hear may sound ridiculous, unfair, or hurtful. It's still better to hear it. Knowledge precedes understanding.

Can you comprehend another's perspective enough to summarize it? To say, "Let me see if I get what you're saying." I know, that sounds like counselor-speak. And it might feel odd at first. As said previously, you don't have to feel like doing something to do it. You do it because it's good to do.

Some starter questions.

Why do you think this?

Why do you think I think this?

How often do I do that?

What am I doing that makes you think or feel that?

What can I do differently?

Will you let me know when I'm doing that?

Asking questions can be risky. The answers may prod you to defend yourself. Ask first, answer later.

Seeking to understand softens another. It says, "I'm not here to fight. I'm here to hear." People want to be understood. That itself can tone down an argument.

"You *always* think your way is the best way." "You *never* consider my feelings." How-to-communicate manuals always—oops, *routinely*—warn against flinging absolutes. Rightly so. Who *always* acts badly toward another? Who *never* treats another decently? Absolute accusations are fighting words, screaming for retaliation. *Never* use them. *Always* pursue particulars.

"I'm not the only one who sees this in you." "Your sister feels the same way I do." "I could name a lot of people who agree with me." Ouch, ouch, and ouch. Dirty communication tricks: Cite witnesses. Name allies, others who I think back me up, thus shifting the argument from "me versus you" to "we versus you."

Citing witnesses is an unfair tactic on several levels.

1. My witness may not support me as much as I think. Perhaps he has listened to my side quietly and I heard his silence to be agreement.
2. Should he find out I called him into my dispute, he may be more than a little annoyed or upset.
3. Citing names can result in lingering damage. After hearing what another supposedly thinks of me, how will that now damage his and my relationship? The repercussions are unpredictable. Calling in witnesses may sound as if it

bolsters one's stand, but it comes with a heavy cost to everyone involved.

When the highway ahead is blocked, finding an exit is a good move. When an argument is accelerating toward gridlock, finding exits is likewise a good move.

Wise words from an anonymous source: "His thoughts were slow; his words were few, and seldom formed to glisten. But he was well liked by all his friends. You should have heard him listen."

Overcorrecting

A nineties sitcom wrapped its plots around the everyday interplay of three generations—grandparents, parents, and children. The grandparents' marriage was marked by the mutual mindset "You're wrong." With the twist of a sentence, a talkfest could descend into a bickerfest.

At breakfast, one spouse reached for a fork to halve an English muffin. Annoyed, the other grabbed the fork, chiding that muffins come pre-split and that using a fork is a waste of time. Comeback: The splits are uneven and not all the way through. Those people should put forks in the package. Rebuttal: Those people are professionals, and they split muffins better than you do. In short order, the meal melee heated into a biting "Why do you always think you're right?"

A detail duel can toast the simplest exchange.

HUSBAND. I can't believe I got the lawn mowed before dark.

WIFE. It's been dark for twenty minutes, and you just walked in here.

HUSBAND. It wasn't completely dark. I could still see where I was going.

WIFE. How? You would have been done over an hour ago if you had started at 7:00, like you said you were going to.

HUSBAND. I did. I walked into the garage a few minutes after 7:00.

WIFE. A few minutes after 7:00? I don't know how you tell time, but the clock in here said 7:15 when the mower started up.

HUSBAND. That's because I couldn't get it started right away, and I had to put gas in it.

WIFE. It always starts up. You said that's why you bought it. I looked right at the clock when the mower started, and it was no more than three minutes after you went outside.

HUSBAND. It couldn't have been only three minutes. It takes longer than that to move the mower out.

WIFE. Well, maybe it wouldn't if you kept the garage clean.

About the only thing more tiresome than reading this sort of bicker bout is being a player in it. Or overhearing it. Chronic bickerers can get so absorbed in their wrangling that they're oblivious to how it's agitating others nearby.

Correcting another's story when he's talking to an audience accuses him, not so subtly, of embellishing or, worse, deception.

> SPOUSE A. I took my nephew with me to this year's classic car show. He's getting to the age where he's interested in cars—he's fourteen now.
>
> SPOUSE B. He's not fourteen yet. He won't be fourteen until next month.
>
> SPOUSE A. Well, anyway, he's been asking me for months to take him.
>
> SPOUSE B. I heard him ask you only once, and that was only in the last few weeks.
>
> SPOUSE A. Every time he's here, he asks me.
>
> SPOUSE B. That's probably because he's more interested in the food there than the cars.

The story can have two endings: (1) Tiring of being edited, the narrator goes silent, wanting to salvage what remains of his credibility; (2) with each correction, his irritation mounts. What began as his personal anecdote deteriorates into an edgy exchange.

"What's wrong with a good-natured back-and-forth?" Nothing, as long as both stay good-natured about it. When only one does, the sport is one-sided. Another's initial reaction—her words, tone, demeanor—is a signal whether to keep playing.

A common give-and-take happens between two guys one-upping each other over the fastest route from point A to point B.

FORD. I've gone your way. It has two more stoplights, and they're long ones.

CHEVY. Yeah, but your way has a slower speed limit and heavy police patrol.

FORD. My way has two lanes.

CHEVY. But it also has more traffic, with construction.

EASEL. Hey, I just heard you two guys from the other room. You want to really know the best way to get there?

Ford and Chevy keep honking that their route will shave a good thirty seconds off a four-mile trip. A good-natured banter can take a left turn if "I'm right" becomes a passenger, though.

A critical distinction: Correction—as in good guidance given or taken—is indispensable to personal maturation. Social and moral growth are stunted without it. Such is not the type of correction warned against here, whose aim is not so much to help but to set another straight in matters of little or no significance.

"If someone questions my deepest beliefs, I will correct him." Understandably, but again, this is not quibbling. It is answering a direct objection. Even so, it still raises the question: When is enough? Overcorrecting someone in major or minor matters doesn't typically make for a meeting of the minds. More often, it makes for a banging of the heads. When correction clarifies, correct. When it quibbles, disconnect the correction. Were another wanting resolution, it would have happened many corrections ago.

"Pick your battles" is a child-rearing mantra. Whether it's a helpful mantra or not depends. It's helpful when advising: Overlook behavior that's not wrong. It is not moral misconduct, defiant, hurtful, irresponsible, or dangerous. It is kid junk, the stuff of growing up.

An illustration: Little Eve likes bedtime (she may need to be evaluated). She sings offkey while lying there playing finger puppets until she dozes off. Is she being disobedient? Is she doing anything wrong? Is her sleep-ritual battle worthy?

"Pick your battles" misguides when advising: Act on important moral or social matters, but let slide trivial ones. Eve's brother, Conan, has mouth-control "issues," to co-opt reigning psychobabble. When he "only" rolls his eyes at you, punctuated with a huffy "Whatever," stand down. It's just piddly teen posturing.

Conversely, while screaming at you, Conan is also kicking chairs. Say the experts: Now intervene. Chair-kicking is major. Eye-rolling is minor. Whatever! In your eyes, are both disrespectful? If yes, then you decide what is major and what is minor. The standards are yours, not Dr. Yule Feelgood's.

"Pick your battles" works well adult to adult. Before disputing another, ask yourself: How important is this really? Now? Tomorrow? Ever? Why am I feeling compelled to correct?

A brand-new word is bristling its way through our lexicon: "microaggression." It's the act of saying anything—however minor or benign—that anyone anywhere anytime finds offensive. Of course, how can one always predict who will find what offensive? The word captures the culture's growing peevishness, and it is the absolute antithesis of unoffendability.

A related word—one I have just coined—is "microcorrection." Unlike a detail duel, it is an immediate correction of one's pronunciation, language, or recall.

Suppose someone uses "laxadaisical" or "off-ten." Microcorrection: "It's lackadaisical" or "Did you mean to say 'often'?"

"I remember where I was on 9/11. It was a Wednesday morning." Microcorrection: "It was a Tuesday."

Is microcorrecting a microcompulsion, like noticing a slightly askew wall picture and feeling the urge to level it? Jumping on a miniscule misspeak can make another feel inept. It can say, "I don't make those kinds of mistakes" or "I'm smarter than that."

Radio talk-show hosts work beside a computer monitor that lists the waiting caller's name, location, and question or comment. "Let's go to Ford from Detroit." Occasionally, the host will use the wrong name, whereupon he'll be corrected—"It's Forbes." Neither the host nor any listener knows who Ford, a.k.a. Forbes, is. Why the "get it right"? The radio host feels no major mistake, as the setting is anonymous. The same can't be said with a face-to-face correction.

Matching a corrector word for word is tempting. His know-it-all attitude provokes. Again, the question: What do you gain? Does he come around to your view? Do you widen his perspective? At correction number 12, do you hear, "I never really looked at it like that"?

I think I'm correct: Most people don't like to be corrected, not repeatedly anyway. What's more, those most resistant to correction routinely do the most correcting.

When you do correct, weigh the topic. Is it worthwhile? Or is it trifling—like muffins, mowers, and motorways?

Instructive, Constructive, Destructive

Albert Einstein observed that time is relative. It can seem to speed up or slow down depending upon one's perspective. Einstein was talking physics. Time is relative also when talking criticism.

Tell me what you think are my positives, and the minutes fly. I welcome feedback, so long as it's approval.

Point out my negatives, and time slows. Hurry up; right now I'd rather be almost any other place.

All criticism is not created equal. It speaks in distinct voices—instructive, constructive, and destructive.

Instructive if given to shape a skill. For example, playing the piano—"Glide your fingers more smoothly. With less frenzy." Or writing—"Less repetition. More clear, compact sentences." Okay, I hear you.

Instructive criticism is repetitive. It can be relentless. Yet the learner accepts it, seeks it. Why? Because it's aimed toward mastery, not toward him. Were it aimed toward him—"Your movements on the keyboard show a real lack of coordination" or "Your writing is a sign of a fuzzy thinker"—it would risk rejection. Moving from instruction to personal loses pupils fast.

Coaches watch skilled players walk away when their mentoring is wrapped with meanness. Bad tone drowns out good training.

As long as criticism stays instructive, it is safe to give and to get.

Constructive is delivered likewise to benefit. "Constructive" is more often used by the giver, however, than by the receiver.

A grandmother laments the growing distance between her and her daughter with children. Do you give advice about her parenting? "Yes, but only to be helpful." Does she ask for it? "No." How often do you give it? "Less now, as she's not taking it as help but more as criticism." Do you mean it as criticism? "Not at all." But she thinks you're questioning her motherhood? "I guess so."

"Doesn't Taylor need a warmer coat today?" "I don't think Sherlock understands why he can't have that." "Joy just wants more hugs and kisses." Grandma may genuinely mean to mentor, but she may not be so heard.

Someone's reaction to a first-time constructive comment tells how she'll react to it a second time or a third and so on. When correction is welcomed, repetition reinforces. When not, it meets more resistance.

Grandma's fix: No "help" given unless asked. If asked, have daughter sign a permission form to speak. Just kidding—sort of.

Commit to change. "I'm sorry for coming across as if I'm questioning you. I promise it won't happen anymore. You're the parent, not me. I had my turn." And for sure, don't add, "And I see I didn't do such a good job either." Now that would be destructive criticism.

"You can do better than to take that job." "You're trying again for another child? Aren't you busy enough?" "I would never buy one of Guarendi's books." My rough estimate is that 61.235 percent of constructive criticism is not "What you're doing is wrong or immoral." It is "That's not the way I would do it." Or "That's not how I think."

Your daughter, Telly, is the only ninth grader in her class without the latest, greatest smartphone. (There's a misnomer.) To hear her, she's the only ninth grader in the Western Hemisphere so deprived. The critiques come: "That's how kids socialize these days." "Telly will feel isolated from her friends." "You'll teach her to be sneaky." You disagree on all counts. Telly's having access to the immediate universe—its good, bad, and vile—in her palm is an immediate risk, socially and emotionally.

Are you doing anything wrong? In whose hands is this decision? Who knows Telly best? Are you wanting to parent by consensus?

"You should see it my way" is not constructive criticism. It is comparison criticism. "You need to be more like me" doesn't automatically result in "You'll be better for it."

In medicine, the correct dosage, often measured in cubic centimeters—cc's—can cure. Too many can harm, even end life. Too many cc's—constructive criticisms—can harm, even end a relationship.

When criticizing, however well-meaning, err on the side of less. The most open-minded person can be overdosed.

Destructive, as the name says, can destroy a relationship, sometimes with only a few words. It smacks of "I'll tell you what is wrong with you. Hope it doesn't hurt too much."

Stinging swipes may or may not be accurate. Accuracy is not their main intent, however. Personal assault is. They come with a noticeable mean streak.

While constructive criticism can court defensiveness, destructive criticism almost always guarantees it. Its nastiness nullifies any legitimacy.

"He needs to hear what he's like." "She has no idea how she comes across, so she needs to be told." "He's quick to criticize. Let's see how he likes getting criticized." Calling destructive criticism instructive doesn't ease its burn. A rose by any other name …

Before verbally smacking, think: What's my purpose? To hurt? Retaliate? Provoke? How much will it sear the relationship? For how long? Temporarily? Permanently? Will this always be my opinion?

"He thinks he's superior." "Her motto is, 'I'm right, you're not.'" "He acts like he's better than everybody else."

Critical people have oversized egos, right? Actually, just the opposite is mostly true. Their egos aren't inflated; they're fragile. Talking another down is their way of talking themselves up.

When you recognize that someone's criticism is rooted in insecurity, it doesn't hit as hard. His attempt to demean says more about him than about you. After a while, you may even start to feel a bit sorry for him. Okay, I did say "after a while."

Criticism hits hardest those closest: spouses, parents, children. Once more, the law of social proximity rules: Daily contact raises more chances for friction. "I love you" and "I'm quick to criticize you" unfortunately can coexist in the same relationship.

A talkative lady interrupts me during our monthly church group gatherings, but I don't correct her. She averages three interruptions per hour—an ignorable number.

My spouse interrupts me, too, and well over three times a month. I've reminded her, not always so calmly, hundreds of times. Hyperbole? Two per week equals one hundred per year. Would adding another hundred or so quiet the problem? Would correction number 1,763 finally halt our cycle of "You interrupt; I get upset"? Or would it just keep scraping this long-time marriage sore spot? Which is the better solution: To let most interruptions pass or to confront each and every one? Ironically, ignoring may actually slow the habit quicker than continuous criticism.

A discipline law: The more parents nag, the less they're heard. Kids instinctively tune out reiterated words. A criticism law: The more one criticizes, the less he's heard. Reiterating words lose potency.

"If I don't say something, somebody will think it doesn't bother me." Have you never said anything? Or have you said the same endlessly? Ongoing criticism trends toward futility. It all too often invokes comeback criticism.

Heavy rain pelting hard ground digs meandering water trenches. With more rain, the water runs faster, cutting deeper. So too with criticism. The faster it flows, the deeper it cuts.

To slow the flow, give heavy emotion time to taper. When you most feel the urge to lash out, delay, if only for seconds. What feels a near overwhelming impulse will ease just enough to allow a little more self-control. (More to come about severing the link between fevered emotions and harsh words.)

One technique for weight reduction is intermittent fasting. The strategy is simple: No eating at set times—for example, before noon and after 6:00 p.m. Or nothing after 3:00 p.m. until breakfast. Limited eating breaks the habit of anytime eating.

Intermittent fasting can break the habit of anytime criticism. For example, no criticizing before noon and after 6:00 p.m. Or no criticism after 7:00 p.m. until morning. Sleep allows several quiet hours. No-criticism zones can slowly be lengthened. Intermittent food fasting limits what goes into the mouth. Intermittent criticism fasting limits what comes out of the mouth.

Marriage-mending gurus suggest "date nights" for spouses to reconnect. One study added a qualifier: Date nights don't reconnect if day times disconnect. That is, "I don't want to go out with you for two hours a week if you don't talk to me with respect the rest of the week." Cut the criticism. Then make the dinner reservation.

Instructive—the safest type of criticism. As long as it centers on the skill being taught and doesn't get personal, it is constructive.

Constructive—its benefit lies in its accuracy, style, and motive. "Constructive" is all too often a code word for "This is what I think you need to change."

Destructive—living down to its name, it destroys relationships. Insults and personal attacks are its ammunition. It does little but hurt, both the criticizer and the criticizee.

Being open to legitimate criticism fosters personal maturity. Discounting any and all criticism fosters personal regression. However well presented, though, criticism is often not well accepted. Therefore, be slow to criticize, even if you only mean to help, even if you believe someone needs to hear it, even if you believe he deserves it.

The Off-Putters

Bragging, complaining, know-it-all-ing—all have the same effect. They put people off. In small doses, they can undo a conversation. In large doses, they can undo a relationship.

Most relationships have pieces of these. That's normal communication. The risk lies in the frequency. The more they intrude, the more distance they put.

Bragging: promoting one's competence, achievements, or status—or those of one's offspring. How boastful something sounds depends upon its audience. Grandma beams over Dad's regaling her with Stanford's all-As report card. She can't wait to frame it and regale her friends with her brainiac grandson. Dad's cousin, whose daughter is a nuclear particle physicist, smiles politely but isn't all that impressed. And to Dad's brother, whose son last saw an A three years ago, it's a hurting reminder.

Self-speak sounds louder when someone isn't all that fond of the speaker. It rapidly grows tiresome. So, if you're tempted to brag, make sure it's to someone who likes you.

Common impulses for bragging: to impress, to win approval, to gain respect, to feel superior.

Talking superior, however, may compensate for feeling inferior. A bragger elevates himself because of self-doubts. In his mind, he doesn't measure up. Thus, his message is not "I think I'm better than you" but rather "I don't think I'm as good as you." It is insecurity rather than ego that moves him.

Bragging may show competition. Someone who considers you more talented, admired, or respected than he is may feel the urge to spotlight himself. In his eyes, you're impressive, so he's proclaiming, "Me too." He raises himself to compete with you. It's not because you started the competition, is it?

Bragging obeys the law of diminishing returns. The more self-talk, the less credibility. It provokes skepticism. How much of what's said is exaggeration? Fact and fiction blur.

Bragging closes ears. Others stop listening, sooner rather than later. Acquaintances and casual friends are among the first to tune out. A good rule when first meeting others: Don't tell them who you are. Let them find out for themselves. They'll remember it longer.

Complaining: dwelling upon one's troubles, disappointments, and pains. Another good social rule: Don't burden others with your problems. Many don't care, and a few are glad you have them.

Some do care, though, because they care about you. You hurt, so they do too. At that, even those closest to you don't have a bottomless well for woe-talk. A little might evoke sympathy; a lot is monotonous or depressing, especially when it comes with no interest in solutions. The country song sums it: "You can feel bad if it makes you feel better."

Chronic complaining is a fixation: "Life or others are not treating me right." Granted, life and others don't always treat anyone right. That is life behaving this side of Heaven. Expecting life and others always to act in our interests is a credo for complaining.

Like bragging, complaining lands heavier on some ears than on others. A mother, overcome with grief over her nine-year-old daughter's death from leukemia, spoke of her unexpected reaction: a diminished tolerance for others' complaining, especially about minor annoyances and disappointments. A hard workday, a surprise repair, or—most biting—child-rearing frustrations did not evoke empathy but a silent "Please stop." How another perceives complaining depends upon what life has handed her.

A colleague scheduled a meeting with a company's executive, someone he had never met. Upon entering his office, he found him with his back turned, looking out the window. The executive asked, "Ron, have you ever had a really bad day?" Perplexed by the odd greeting, Ron replied, "I suppose almost everyone has." Swiveling around, the man revealed a badly burned, heavily scarred face. "Ron,

I too thought I had bad days until I had a truly bad day. That one day put it all in perspective for me."

An earlier chapter's theme: People are attracted to those who are interested in them. Supporting someone in his troubles shows interest. When woe-talk is a steady theme, however, being a good listener isn't always good. Empathizing with another's single-minded gloom may initially seem kind, but the guiding question is: Am I helping or hurting? It is caring to listen. It is also caring to know when to stop listening.

Professional speakers follow the rule: Know your audience. Bragging and complaining follow the same rule. While some do want to know all about your life—including its highs and lows—others shrink from self-talk or woe-talk. And some think, "Want to trade troubles?"

Know-it-all-ing: Someone with special expertise is not called a know-it-all; he's better called a know-all-about-it. And unless he belittles those less knowing, his competence is respected.

On the other hand, "know-it-all" is a label reserved for someone who speaks with authority but who lacks understanding or knowledge. On diverse subjects, he's convinced he knows lots and is ever ready to convince others of that, too. The adage is: None hold an opinion so surely as the uninformed.

So what if the know-it-all talks as if he knows more than he actually does? Why is that so bothersome? Because know-it-all-ing comes with correction. Whereas bragging says, "Let me tell you all about me," know-it-all-ing says,

"Let me tell you all about why I'm right" and therefore "why you are wrong."

Someone who speaks so, in effect, is bragging about his supposed smarts. Whatever the topic—religion, morals, politics, parenting, cliff diving—he presents himself as better informed than you. Take a lesson from him: Your reaction to him is how others would react to you were you to talk likewise.

"Why doesn't he see that he does the same things he accuses others of doing?" Psychologists talk of an "ego defense" called projection. It is seeing in others what we ourselves do.

Rather than a self-defense, projection can be a self-help. If I'm hyperattuned to anyone's bragging, is it possible I, too, self-promote? If, after hearing only two sentences I tag you a know-it-all, is this a sign I'd best keep a rein on my own overinflated opinions? The shortcomings I am quick to see in others may be telling me to scrutinize myself.

High on the list of conversation killers are bragging, complaining, and know-it-all-ing. Few of us can erase every trace of these in our speech. But the more we do, the more others will find us winsome and enjoyable.

Welcome Insults?

"Blessed are you when men revile you and ... utter all kinds of evil against you falsely on my account. Rejoice and be glad" (Matt. 5:11–12).

The words of Jesus, who Christians believe is the God-Man, from His Sermon on the Mount. One needn't be a Christian, though, to benefit from His words.

Neutralizing insults and offenses is a theme of this book. Ignore, expect, deflect—all ways to weaken their wallop.

Jesus is speaking of a particular brand of insults—those aimed at the beliefs and morals of His followers. He says to be glad to receive them. What's more, He adds: *Rejoice* over evil words aimed at you. *Rejoice?*

Is this humanly possible? Is it beyond our emotional limits? Jesus obviously doesn't think so. He wouldn't enjoin us to do something we couldn't do. As God, He knows our limitations, more so than we do.

He doesn't just say: Ignore scorn; don't let someone's acid words burn you. He says: Welcome them. Be glad you're hearing them because of me.

Couldn't some insults be deserved? Is every one of them unjust? Couldn't some have merit, not because of my Faith but because of my manner?

In my thirties, I drifted from the Catholic Church, the church of my youth, and moved for a time into an independent congregation. A recurrent question in our Sunday Bible study: "Why do some people get so upset over our moral principles?" A recurrent answer: Those principles convict them. Somewhere deep down, those people know that those principles are right.

Morals that oppose the culture's will agitate many. Flickering inside them may still be a God-placed sense of right and wrong. Theologians call this the natural law.

Still, I wondered, is it my convictions that bother others, or could something less virtuous also be present? Others' maligning me for believing in God-given standards is to be expected. My maligning those who ignore His standards is to be rejected. One can be morally upright and still be a jerk about it. Am I "holy" or "holier than thou"?

If charged with spiritual elitism, whom do I first look at? Me or my accuser? Do I ask myself, "Is he right?" Is there a log blocking my vision or, in psych-speak, my self-awareness?

A wise nun said, "If others dislike me because of Jesus, that's good. If they dislike Jesus because of me, that's bad."

When another's words are ignorant, unfair, or malicious, to think, "He doesn't know what I've been given to know. If he did, he'd talk differently. I will pray he comes to know"—in boxing lingo, this is slipping the punch. Prayer for and ill will toward another can't exist together. They are antagonists.

Jesus knows social truth: For someone's words to really upset me (again, assuming they're untrue), I have to cooperate. I have to allow them to really upset me. The intensity of my reaction is self-determined. Granted, lowering my emotional barometer takes repetition, but in time, formerly hard-hitting words will lose force.

Jesus' teaching sounds quite foreign in a society that urges: "If people are offensive, be offended. If they talk bad to you, feel bad." The society is nowhere near as smart as Jesus.

I can't control another's mouth, but I can control my ears. If not, I will live hoping others will speak well to me. "They shouldn't have said that" surges my emotions. "They shouldn't, but they did" eases them. Forty-plus years as a therapist has taught me that most of us greatly underestimate our ability to mitigate insults.

Jesus knows that you and I possess that ability. He doesn't merely instruct: Don't let others' criticism disturb you because you're my follower. He says much more: Turn their criticism to compliments. That is doable. The God-Man says so. Unless, that is, I'm more offended when I'm insulted than when He is.

Snark Remarks

"Snarky": having a rudely critical tone or manner. Synonyms: "snippy," "snitty," "snotty," "snooty," "snarly." The "sn" sound seems to precede all sorts of snappy sneers.

"You're thoughtless." However trait-talking, the charge is straight-talking. It is snideless. "Well, I see you're thinking about somebody else for a change. Wait, let me mark that on my calendar." Now that reeks of snide.

"Do you have to yell?" is likewise blunt, but it speaks to the present, a right-now behavior. "Oh, you can actually talk in a civil tone, at least when it suits you." A snark can summon the past, as in, "This is how you always act."

Snarks can be self-satisfying. Because there is witticism to the criticism, as the sender hears it anyway, he can feel smug about his cleverness. His sharp-edged zinger convinces him, "I won that round."

Snarks reverberate. They echo in the ears, linger in the head. Like an inkblot test, they invite interpretation.

"What exactly did that mean?" "Is that slam what she really thinks?" "And just why should I read that book *How to Get Along with* Almost *Everybody?*"

Snarks arouse wariness, an uneasy vigilance. When am I going to get stuck with another of these jabs? What topics do I need to shun? An isolated snipe can be shrugged off as "out of character." Repeated snipes can't. They corrode a relationship. Backhanded remarks rankle even more than direct criticism.

"You just don't listen!" can come from frustration. "It's a good thing your ears hold up your glasses. They don't get used for much else"—also from frustration, but with an added twist of lemon. It has the sound of premeditation.

Recall the example of the perpetrator of a heinous crime. During the trial, a group advocating mercy gathered outside the courthouse. Exiting the building, the accused smirked and flicked a digital sign of disdain at them. His snark was silent, but it had enough power to provoke some to rethink their pleas for mercy.

Silent snarks—eye rolls, huffy sighs, head movements—without words say, "Yeah, right. You're ridiculous." "That's nonsense" may actually be less provocative than a peevish eye roll. People don't take well to disdain, spoken or unspoken.

A young woman's family accused her of embracing her Christian faith too deeply along with being judgmental of them. Do you comment? "No." Do you say anything that sounds judgmental? "I don't think so." Any other signs of judgment? "I've rolled my eyes at some things they say." Her face was prompting their "You're judgmental." I cautioned her: Keep your eyes to yourself.

One challenge to learning English is that meaning may lie not only in words but in tone. "That's just fine" can mean "That's totally acceptable" or "That's totally unacceptable," depending upon the inflection. "Thank you very much" can say, "I'm real grateful" or "I'm real displeased," depending upon the tone. "Good for you" can convey approval or disapproval. Everyday language can be positive or negative, depending solely upon how it's expressed.

A snark doesn't need ugly words to bruise. It can take good words and wrap them with ugliness.

My elderly Italian aunt had an agile mind and could summon up a quick *riposte*. At being dismissed as an immigrant by a woman proclaiming "true American" ancestry, my aunt coolly replied, "You do look like you came over on the *Mayflower*."

"I can't think that fast." That's good. It's a safeguard. Even should you want to, the words are hard to conjure. While a mental replay may spur "I should have said . . . ," be glad you didn't. Some remarks are better left unsaid, whether from self-restraint or lack of quick-enough thinking.

What if you can think that fast? Maybe that's because you're just better at seeing others' faults than your own? Ooops—that just slipped out. Sorry. Do some self-analysis. At whom would you be most likely to fling a cheap shot? When? Why? To put her "in her place"? To poke your point? To slap down a dispute? To act superior? To show yourself quick-witted? To imply, "Don't mess with me. In a war of words, you're unarmed."

It might feel like a short-term win, but at what cost? Will you be heard as savvy or snotty? Will you set others around you on edge? Will you score the points you thought you'd score?

Snarks close ears and minds. Even if your point has merit, it is buried by the tone. To borrow the title of a popular book, snarks aren't "How to Win Friends and Influence People."

Snarks may reveal insecurities. They often tell more about the sender than the receiver. Another's pulling you down is a way to pull himself up. Hearing them this way should lessen their bite.

When being snarked, you could just look puzzled, as if to say, "I don't get what you mean." A lack of reaction conveys, "Say it outright."

My wife had a friend who occasionally struck with a snark. After hearing a few of these, my wife would respond, "Ouch!" The snarks faded.

A strong aversion to feeling demeaned or disparaged is wired into us. It's an innate protection of the self. Snarks pelt at that protection, and too many can snip the ties of a relationship.

Petty Peeves

"Don't sweat the petty things, and don't pet the sweaty things." A life rule from the comedian George Carlin.

Petty: "Of little or no importance or consequence"—the dictionary definition. The relationship definition depends upon who is doing the defining. What is minor to one may be major to another. Of little consequence in the doer's eyes may be big in the receiver's. Petty is in the eye of the beholder.

One thing is sure: The more annoyances one defines as small, the less time he spends being peeved.

Pre-marriage, I lived as a neatnik. Post-marriage with ten children forced me to markedly relax my standards. God has a sense of humor. Stressing myself over a child's definition of order would have kept me locked in a state of perpetual disorder.

Early in marriage, as my wife and I were learning each other's daily ways, cupboard doors routinely stood open, and not by my hand. As a highly trained professional, employing savvy communication techniques (I-messages, not you-messages) I should have adeptly resolved this minor matter. Apparently, my skills needed fine-tuning, as the doors gradually crept back open.

To paraphrase the axiom: A picture is worth a thousand nags, or, as I preferred to call mine, reminders. One morning, seeing seven of twelve doors agape (but who's petty enough to count?), I opened the other five, calculating that would take less energy than closing seven—a net gain of two. When Randi walked in, her shocked look said, "I know I didn't do all that." She also knew only one other person could have. Without a word, she closed all twelve.

On one hand, I felt pretty juvenile. On the other, I assumed the image would speak for itself. Apparently not. Days and open doors later, I finally scolded myself: "Ray, just close them." So I did, though perhaps a bit loud, as a neighbor called asking, "Is someone lighting firecrackers in your kitchen?"

After all this, I looked at me instead of at the doors. "Am I being petty or what?" First of all, left-open cupboards deserve little grousing in the bigger marital scheme of things, even less so as kids enter the scene, bringing with them left-on lights, dripping faucets, and muddy shoes.

Second, to use a football analogy, in marrying Randi, I had outkicked my coverage. Meaning, she was a giving spouse well beyond me. Her positive qualities dwarfed any meaningless "negative" ones, such as leaving doors ajar. Would she say, I wonder, that she had outkicked her coverage?

Third, I had personalized the whole cupboard caper. Instead of realizing what it really was—forgetfulness—I thought, "I've asked nicely. Doesn't it matter what I want here?" The doors had nothing to do with me, but I made them so. Where's a psychologist when I need one?

My last solution, which should have been my first, was to close the doors myself, quietly, without counting. In fact, once I shut my mouth, more doors were shut. Two lessons for me: (1) quit badgering someone, and her habit may taper on its own; and (2) quit being a jerk.

Long-time successful marriages know: Don't get riled over the little stuff. They also know: More stuff is little.

To keep small stuff small, recognize: Every personality has its own habits and quirks, which can be durable and unconscious. What's more, most personalities share the same quirk: One's own foibles are seen as smaller than others'.

Next, pay attention: What are this person's good points and attributes? The more plusses, the less focus to give any tiny minus. Spouses can get yanked into a spiral of bickering over the same peeves: socks on the floor, water splashed on the mirror, ownership of the remote, a snorting laugh. A small irksome way can reverberate loudly throughout the whole relationship, becoming a focal point for emotional skirmishes.

Final questions: How long will I agitate myself about this? How much of my time and energy will I let it steal?

Weeks? Months? Years? Has my reaction settled anything or just made for more collisions?

"I'm not asking much. Why can't she change for me?" Do as I say, not as I did with the doors. Don't personalize. Most minor habits are more due to forgetting, inattention, or oversight and less due to deliberate disregard. To personalize them is to fill them with too much meaning.

Psychologists talk about "negativity bias." It is noticing the bad more than the good, the wrong more than the right. News programs chase ratings by feeding into this bias, promoting the uglier stories up front. The negative grabs our attention, in both media and in relationships.

"If I don't say something, it'll just keep happening." How often have you said something? My close-the-door saying somethings totaled upward of twenty or more. While relatively few, compared with the kinds of numbers that can accumulate in a relationship over time, my couple of dozen could still be called nagging.

Who likes being nagged or badgered? We either resist or we tune out. Even if giving credence to the nag, at some point we refuse to budge, especially if we see the matter as no big deal. Saying nothing sometimes speaks loudest.

"If I don't say anything, she'll think it doesn't bother me." Isn't that the aim—to not let it bother you? Your history shows it bothers you. Silence breaks the cycle.

All here is not to say: Everything—big or little—is best downplayed. It is to caution against making little matters big. Little matters only get bigger when endlessly belabored.

You define "petty." You give meaning to everyday annoyances. Their presence doesn't automatically have to color a relationship. How much they intrude is up to you.

Petting the sweaty things can leave your hand sticky, if not stinky. Sweating the petty things can leave a relationship sticky, if not stinky.

Just Ignore It

All I Really Need to Know I Learned in Kindergarten[1] is a bestseller dispensing witty wisdom from the sandbox through the counselor's office. Nothing too academic, just some basics for more grown-up living. A sampler: Share, play fair, don't hit, clean your mess, flush, take a nap (liking it more).

I learned nothing in kindergarten for one reason: I wasn't there. It wasn't yet required. My kids were convinced I walked straight into a one-room schoolhouse. First grade did teach me some lifelong social lessons, though.

A schoolmate decided I needed a more fitting name: Short Boy. Not a complete surprise, as my ancestry is Italian, and we are not a tall people. To neutralize his move, I turned to a trusty kid comeback: "I'm rubber, you're glue. Whatever you say bounces off me and sticks to you. No

[1] Robert Fulghum, Ivy Books, 1989.

reversies!" Adding "No reversies" is critical. Otherwise, the boy could counter, "Reversies," and I'd be stuck being the glue. It's schoolyard code. Apparently, he didn't fear being sticky because he continued to mouth the diminutive moniker.

My mother did some damage control. "You're only six. You have years to grow." "A person's real height is from the neck up." *Huh?* I thought. Mom was barely five feet tall. Good thing first grade didn't teach a course on genetics.

"If he won't stop, you may just have to ignore it." That's it? That's what I should do? Just ignore it? I suppose I can do that. After all, moms know about these things.

Ignoring it did shortly silence him. Ironically, he was only slightly taller than I. Therapists would call his taunting projection.

Somewhere between kidhood and adulthood, however, the counsel to ignore what is best ignored gets ignored. It sounds too simple, too juvenile. A grown-up reflexively asks, "How do I do that?" A six-year-old doesn't. He just starts ignoring. Then again, having in reserve "I'm rubber, you're glue" does help.

Ignore means: Say nothing. Saying something admits, "I heard that!" To ignore is to look as if you didn't hear what, in fact, you did.

Kids are naturals at doing this. It's their default defense against a parent's outrageous demands. "Dawn, you didn't make your bed yet, and I've asked you four times." "Why is your coat still on the floor, Taylor, after I've told you over and over to hang it up?" "I didn't hear you." It's selective hearing loss (SHL). Do you know a first grader? Maybe he could teach you how to ignore.

Suppose a snippy remark is impossible to ignore, the eye contact being too direct. Implement plan B—situation-specific bewilderment (SSB). Look as if you're not sure what the snip means. Columbo, the television detective, was a master of SSB. As a suspect foisted upon him a dubious story, he looked perplexed and followed with, "Just one thing I don't understand . . ."

Children, teens more so, stand primed to debate a parent's rules. And the more we explain, the more they debate. At some point—sooner rather than later—a parent's best response is no response, just a look saying, "I don't know what more to say." A dumb look can be very smart.

A well-known shoe company has watched its sales soar with a simple slogan: Just do it. Apparently this three-word prescription has people jumping into their shoes.

"Just do it" answers "How?" It is the decision to ignore. It is not "I wish I could"; it is "I will." Does that sound too simple, so simple that a first grader could do it? It is, but simple doesn't mean easy. Practice is what makes simple easier.

How do fitness buffs stay buff? Some days, the couch's siren call can get pretty enticing. If they vacillate—"Should I just skip exercising today?"—the couch could tempt, "Sit here and think about it." They've learned not even to begin the debate but to ignore the couch and to head for exercise. In short, they just do it.

Age six, for me, was a lifetime ago. Truth is, this is as old as I've ever been. Why do I find my mother's advice harder to follow now—when I'm older and supposedly smarter—than then?

One explanation: mental rehearsal—a feeling-fueled inner dialogue. Someone wrongs us, as we see it anyway. We analyze. "How could she talk to me like that?" We dissect. "Selfish? What exactly does she mean by that?" We refute. "Talk about selfish! Has she ever looked at herself?" We weigh options. "Should I call her? Send her an e-mail? Or wait until it happens again, and then set her straight?"

The self-talk can replay for hours, days even. The provocation comes alive again in our head. A synergy begins. The emotion feeds the rehearsal. And the rehearsal feeds more emotion. The actual trouble spanned minutes, maybe seconds. But ruminating about it can span hours. Rehearsal talks over letting it go.

Your Aunt Angela freely bestows her narrow-minded opinions about others to anyone who will listen. Hearing her, most times you shrug, until yesterday, when she held court around the family table about your narrow-minded religion. Twenty-four hours later, you're still smoldering.

Aunt Angela's diatribe can't "go in one ear and out the other" when it runs headlong into a barrier—your brain, or more precisely, your mind. Your emotions post rant are not automatic, though they may feel so. They need your thoughts to inflame them. The longer you allow Aunt

Angela to live in your head, the longer you'll stay upset. Rehearsal keeps her harangue alive.

Lawyers will tell you that just about anybody can sue just about anybody for just about any reason. That doesn't mean the suit has any merit. That's just the legal reality.

The social reality: Anybody can say anything to you or about you for any reason. That doesn't mean their words have any merit.

Before ignoring someone's words, ask yourself: Do they have any merit? Is what I'm hearing true? The saying is: If you want to make me angry, tell a lie about me. If you want to make me really angry, tell the truth about me.

A lie can be easier to ignore. It doesn't threaten my self-view. The truth can. It says something about me, that somewhere, down deep, I may know but would rather not admit. If something is the truth, it deserves my attention. Otherwise, it does not. Honest self-appraisal can make the distinction.

Working in radio and television, I receive audience feedback. No surprise, but it's not always "Good show. Keep it up." Should I judge that an e-mail was sent to hurt, not help, my response is "delete"—the cyber counterpart of "ignore." Next, I delete it from my mind. Can I always immediately do so? No, but with practice—plenty—the time span between exiting my inbox and exiting my head is getting shorter.

Were my mother alive to read one of those "How did *you* get your own show" missives, I suspect that her mama-bear protective instincts would override her counsel to "just ignore it." A few of them call me worse than "Short Boy."

"If you don't confront a problem, it could get worse." Yes, it could. Therefore, speak up or let slide? One guide is frequency. How recurrent is the problem? If once or a few times, then speaking up has a decent chance at resolution. The sore spot doesn't rule the relationship. It is a contrast to it.

On the other hand, repeatedly confronting trouble invites defensiveness, as in, "Oh yeah, what about you?" How likely are you to hear, "I wasn't aware that I come across that way. Thank you for always making sure to point it out. That makes me a better person"? Uh huh.

A difficult person can be self-myopic. Meaning, he doesn't see himself as difficult. If he did, he'd be less difficult. The longer someone has been difficult toward you, the wiser to confront less and ignore more.

Should you decide to speak up, shun *trait talk*. Trait talk uses broad personality language. "You are *thoughtless*." "You're *selfish*." "You're just *irritable*." Trait talk doesn't say, "This is what you did." It says, "This is who you are." Most people won't accept that an incident or two of poor behavior defines what they are. The more you use trait talk, the more you'll be ignored.

Specific speaks more clearly and with less accusation. "You were late, so I got frustrated." "That remark bothered me." "What did I say that got you so upset?"

To repeat myself—at the risk of being ignored—"Just ignore it" is good counsel for all ages: kindergartners through retirees. It's a skill honed by practice. Applied liberally, it interrupts what could otherwise deteriorate into open conflict. And it's a companion to being more easygoing.

Speak Up or Shut Up

"Self" is a revered word among psychologists. It links up with other revered words: "self-image," "self-esteem," "self-actualization," "self-expression."

Self-expression, in one sense, is telling others—often, if need be—where you stand. It is letting them know clearly what is bothering you about their behavior. Doing so leads to fewer misunderstandings. On paper, the theory sounds sensible; in reality, it doesn't always end so well.

"Authentic self" is a kindred term: "Be who you are with others. Act in harmony with your genuine personhood." If you're not sure exactly what that means, neither am I. It's expressed by the cry "I've got to be me!"

While making for a catchy Sammy Davis Jr. song title, it can make for some sour notes between people.

A friend freely offers his takes on my profession. "What? Who in his right mind wants to listen to troubles all day?" My standard comeback: "I do." As they gather, though, they wear thinner. So I indulge in some self-expression, diplomatically at first. If he understands, problem solved. If not, I express again, only not so diplomatically.

Which one is my authentic self? The forbearing therapist type or the blunt buddy? Both are. Who shows up depends upon the circumstances: whom I'm with, what they say, and how they say it.

Better asked: Which me will foster an easier relationship with my friend, which is what I want?

Is my authentic self the me who speaks my immediate emotions or desires? Or is it me who weighs whether or not to speak? My urge to verbally blister someone may feel truly me at the moment, but another part of me—my mind—says, "Control yourself." Otherwise, real damage can follow.

"Keeping everything inside isn't healthy. Always shutting up is asking for an ulcer." In fact, ulcers are generally caused by bacteria, not pent-up emotions. Of course, calm give-and-take is a cornerstone of mature relationships. The wrinkles come when communication becomes only a replay of the same sore spot, when broaching the subject again and again causes more discord than its resolution.

The first attempt to smooth things typically brings the best chance of hearing, "I didn't realize you felt that way. I'm sorry. I'll try to do better." Or something similarly conciliatory. If at first you succeed, no need to try again.

"If at first you don't succeed, try, try again" may be a good formula for skill-building. It's not always so for relationship building. "What are you saying?" "I don't do that." "You do the same thing." "I was only teasing—don't be so sensitive." The guiding question: Am I gaining or losing, by repeating myself about this matter? If losing, the words of the lizard in a classic commercial are worth heeding: "Let it go, Louie."

Motivational speakers preach: "Be you with others. Don't wear a mask." Sometimes it's good to wear a mask. I put on an "I like you" look around an unlikable uncle. I wear a smiley face at a work gathering I'm enjoying about as much as an IRS audit. The outward me is relaxed and comfortable. The inward me, not so much. Am I masking up? Should I just drop all pretense?

Donning a mask is not necessarily phony or deceptive. In acting counter to negative feelings, you'll often escape the repercussions of their free expression. Who knows? Wear some masks long enough, and they might just become your real face.

"Don't wear a mask" could be translated, "Don't show self-control."

I might counsel a spouse to show more affection, as the other is craving the tiniest morsel of it. He responds, "That's not who I am." He sees affection as acting counter to his true persona. He would be faking it.

Is faking it bad? Or can it be the kinder way to act?

A wife would enhance family harmony by arguing less with her husband's father. She demurs, "I'm just an assertive person." Is assertiveness the go-to response, no matter when and with whomever? Or could it be smarter to adjust her personal style for a greater cause?

The 1970s saw the arrival of a social steamroller called assertiveness training. Shaped in the university, AT (you know something has status when you can call it by its initials) rapidly inserted itself into the public consciousness, sparking a flurry of top-selling books with the "I've got to be me" theme (*Looking Out for #1*, *Your Perfect Right*). AT touts the benefits of claiming one's rights in social settings. To do this is to risk resentment and ugly confrontations.

Assertiveness, no matter how well-trained, is a tough animal to bridle. Too much, too often can morph into pushiness, which can morph into obnoxiousness. In teaching others not to walk on me, I can teach them to walk away from me. Knowing when to be assertive, and when to let some things pass, is social self-confidence.

In ancient Middle Eastern cultures, a slap on the cheek was a severe personal insult. It demanded a sharp response. Jesus instead instructed, "If anyone strikes you on the right cheek, turn to him the other also" (Matt. 5:39). Meaning, don't reflexively feel demeaned. Show the slapper he can't provoke you to wrath or retaliation. Every insult doesn't need to be answered. Maybe Jesus missed Assertiveness 101 in synagogue.

To recap, or to re-express myself:

1. Speak up, if it's the first time or if you judge another will be open to hearing again.
2. If past efforts have failed, future efforts are likely to. Reconfronting the same trouble may only provoke more trouble.

3. Know when to shut up. To repeat Kenny Rogers, "You got to know when to hold 'em."
4. Assertiveness can better or worsen a relationship. Laying aside one's "rights" for the sake of peace is often the more self-possessed move.

Damage Control

"When was the last time you apologized?" Spouses' answers can stretch back pretty far. "During our first date." "When our daughter was in first grade—she's in law school now." "At our wedding rehearsal dinner, I spilled coffee on her napkin and did say, 'Sorry about that.' "

You needn't be a shrink to analyze that giving apologies—from one spouse or both—is about as appealing as a root canal.

Why would words with so much reparative potential be so tough to voice? Even as one knows they are deserved, they catch in the throat.

One explanation is ego protection. What exactly does an "I'm sorry" say? Does it say, "At that time and place I acted wrongly"? Or does it say much more: "I'm incompetent ... or a failure ... or inferior ... or a bad person"? The weightier an apology's meaning, the heavier the words to say.

As the father of ten children, I often prompted, "Say you're sorry." Reluctance followed, as a child scanned the floor while mumbling a barely audible "Sorry."

My son recently instructed his two-year-old Caroline, "Tell Rosie [her four-year-old sister] you're sorry." At which she responded, "You're sorry, Rosie."

Little kids don't load apologies with psychological baggage. They lack the sophistication. Their reticence is more straight forward: "I don't want to say that. I don't know why, but I just don't like the sound of it."

We grown-ups may not like the sound of it either. Kids, though, have an excuse. They are at the front end of socialization. They don't yet understand what good can flow from a few sincere words.

We adults do, but the words can still flow slowly.

"I don't believe I did anything to apologize for." That may sometimes be so. Is it always? Furthermore, as I'm the judge of my innocence, am I an unbiased one? When "I did nothing wrong" is the default defense for denying any fault at any time with anyone, well, I'm sorry, but that's just wrong.

This I know without question: I don't always do right by others. I am not a walking, talking saint. Actually, if I were, I'd be more willing to see and say my transgressions.

Being objective about oneself does not come naturally. Subjectivity is the human inclination. Closing the gap between subjective and objective leads to more apologies. As the poet Robert Burns observed, "Oh, the gift that God would give us to see ourselves as others see us." The question is: Would we want the gift?

PAP—personal apology percentage. This is how wrong one must see himself before apologizing. Typical percentage is 50 or above. That is, I have to judge myself at least as wrong as you before venturing an "I'm sorry." As my PAP improves—meaning lowers—so, too, does my willingness to admit any part. If, as I measure it, your percentage is higher, though, then when you apologize, I will. Maybe.

My uncle is flinging several snide remarks at one of my soft spots—faith, family, haircut. The first couple I shrug off. By number four, I've heard one too many. My retaliation is not only loud but laced with some spicy words for emphasis.

An hour later—okay, a week—I have regrets and ponder apologizing. Yes, he started it. Yes, he kept at it. Yes, I tried to defuse it. Therefore, he should apologize. But what if he doesn't? Then neither do I? Because he instigated it, does that make my reaction right? Understandable maybe, but right? Does his 72 percent fault justify my 28 percent? When one's PAP is less than 50, apologizing tests one's humility.

"My apology would just convince him he's all right and I'm all wrong." He could interpret it that way, but that's not what you're saying. And you can't guide what you say by how much someone might mishear it. "I'm sorry—I shouldn't have used that kind of language." "I was wrong to yell like that." "That remark was uncalled for—forgive me." Your apology is talking particulars. It's not a "You win, I lose."

"I already do most of the apologizing." Whatever your ratio—five apologies to one or twenty to one—your PAP says, “Here’s where I’m wrong,” not “Okay, I’m wrong again.” It replaces “It’s all me” with “It’s some me.”

“He talks a good game.” “Her walk doesn’t match her talk.” “Less words, more action.” Almost everyone agrees: It’s easier to talk good behavior than to do good behavior.

Apologies provide an exception to this rule. If an “I’m sorry” is called for, but the words still lie dormant, then what? On to plan B: Act sorry. Be extra nice and pleasant. That will compensate for my previously poor conduct. Should that still be too demanding, I’ll lower my profile, hoping the everyday flow of life will settle any fallout. Acting sorry can be safer for my ego than saying sorry.

Passing a florist’s shop one day, I heard an inner voice (not my wife’s): “Get Randi flowers.” Someone somewhere once decreed that a single rose is more romantic than a full dozen. I don’t know if I buy that, but it sure is less expensive. “May I have one red rose, please?”

With a knowing grin, the young lady teased, “What did you do?”

Huh? said my face.

“Well, most of the time when guys buy flowers, and it’s not for a birthday or holiday, they’re trying to smooth things over.”

I thought, “That might be so for those other guys, but Randi and I have a very open relationship. She will accept my rose as a rose and not as some fragrant compensation.” Walking into the house, looking like a five-year-old hiding a fistful of dandelions for his mother behind his back, I ceremoniously presented my flower to Randi.

"That's so sweet."

Just as I expected. She saw my gift as an impromptu compliment. Then she added, "Should I know something?"

I asked, "Did you ever work for a florist?"

The most meaningful apologies combine words with action, flowers if necessary.

"I'll apologize, but it won't be accepted." That could be related to the distance between your apologies. If "I'm sorry" is a foreign language to you, isn't some wariness to be expected? The reaction is, "Why are you apologizing this time when the last time was four years ago? I marked it on the calendar."

When meeting skepticism, the impulse is to say more and back off, often in a huff. Why be contrite only to get rebuffed? Why be humble only to get humbled? More frequent apologies do lower skepticism, though. They also raise the chances of an "I'm sorry too."

Reverse the roles. You're the one receiving the apology. It's the second this year. Your ears hear, "I'm sorry," but your mind hears, "I'm sorry, okay? Let's just move on." Listen to your ears. Giving credence doesn't make you gullible. You know the words may or may not be sincere. Nothing is hurt by delaying judgment. Apologies leave fast and return slowly when rejected after three words.

"If you were truly sorry, you'd change." This erroneous belief follows the cycle: Act wrong, apologize, act wrong, apologize, act wrong ... I can truly regret my conduct. Yet no matter my intent to shed it, it clings stubbornly. My remorse is real. My apology is genuine.

Neither guarantees "I'll never do this again." The spirit may be willing, but . . .

Catholics receive the Sacrament of Reconciliation, or, as it is popularly known, Confession. So far this life, I've never begun with "Bless me, Father, for I have . . . well, please just bless me. At my age, I've pretty much conquered most of my sins. I mean, how many decades do I need?"

It's more like "Bless me, Father. Here's my list. It covers most of what I still do." So far, no priest has admonished, "You say you're sorry, but then you still do the same things. It makes me wonder, 'Are you truly sorry?' "

"I'll say sorry, but I don't feel sorry." Child-development types scold: Don't make a child apologize. If he doesn't feel it, he's just mouthing it. His apology is not "authentic." If I didn't do right until I felt it, much that is right for me to do would never get done. Acting well routinely means acting counter to one's desires. Ancient philosophers knew: Act well first; the feelings will follow.

Of course, in the fury of a fracas, one's feelings may be anything but apologetic. Any thought of "I shouldn't be saying this" is overcome by fevered feelings.

What then? Do delayed damage control. Find a good time or place to apologize later. Apologies don't always need to be on the spot. Time gives reason a chance to rule emotions. It allows for a better realization of exactly what to apologize for. Good words lacking good feelings are better than no words at all.

This side of Heaven, it's impossible never to say or do anything hurtful, nasty, snotty, mean-spirited, (enter synonyms here). What's more, much misconduct is not a "once and never again." It repeats itself.

What is said and done can't be unsaid and undone, but a sincere expression of regret and sorrow can always be done. Actually, it can make things better.

To Forgive

What does "to forgive" mean? To forgo retaliation—no eye for an eye? To let go of hurt or anger? To purge resentment? To forget history? To like the unlikable? To love the seeming unlovable?

To forgive, for most, is some blend of these. Whatever it means, one thing is certain: It's a rare relationship that can endure without forgiveness, at least somewhat, at least sometimes, at least from one party.

For the Christian, to live the name is to forgive. It is not a suggestion, a "try to." It is a command, an obligation.

One can't move too many pages through the Bible without meeting another verse about forgiveness. "Forgive us our trespasses as we forgive those who trespass against us. . . . But if you do not forgive others their trespasses, neither will your heavenly Father forgive you" (see Matt. 6:12, 15). In other words, we will be forgiven as much as we forgive. It is conditional.

Christians believe Jesus is the God-Man. Therefore, He perfectly knows the most well-adjusted way to live. Modern social research fully aligns with Jesus' teaching about forgiveness. It is good both for the soul and the psyche. Forgiving has far-reaching benefits, personally and interpersonally. The more at peace with oneself, the more at peace with others.

An analogy: Refusing to forgive another is like ingesting a tiny bit of poison every day and waiting for him to feel its effects. While he has no idea what you're doing to yourself.

To be sure, another's behavior can stretch far beyond difficult or unpleasant to violent, abusive, or threatening. To forgive isn't to put oneself at risk. It isn't to persevere when a relationship seriously threatens one's well-being. One can forgive and still seek distance for her own and others' safety.

At that, most relationships fracture not from pathology but from discord, a buildup of cracks—ugly words, thoughtless conduct, erratic emotions. A steady drip of irritants corrodes the connection, while testing one's limits to forgive.

To forgive needs an object—that is, something to forgive. The offense must be actual and not imagined.

A nothing-to-forgive scenario: My mother-in-law arrives to watch the children on an evening my wife will be out but I'll be home. Sensitive to being seen as an incompetent father (They need to be fed? How often?), I find my wife in our bedroom and remark, "Asking your mom to be here makes me look as if I can't supervise the kids myself."

Wryly, she reminds me that I'm the one who may need the supervision (no argument there) and that she only wanted to give me uninterrupted time to work on my latest book—the one warning against misreading another's motives. She meant no slight at all. It existed only in my head, grounded solidly in mental midair. My thought process: misinterpret, be offended, decide to forgive, find nothing to forgive.

Something tells me this progression unfolds more often than I realize.

Come-and-go personal contacts allow time for irritations to settle. A co-worker known for his "I'm more important than you" demeanor floats through your department every month or so. On 99 percent of your days, you don't see him. Is that enough time to overlook his uppity air? "Overlook" is one way to say "forgive."

Aunt Gale blows into town every year and seems intent on spending an hour or so challenging your wayward political views. Are her annual interrogations far enough apart for you to shrug them off? "Shrug off" is another way to say "forgive."

It is the close relationships that can most stretch our ability to overlook, bear with, and forgive. Those we love most can frustrate us most, chafe our feelings fast, and test the limits of our patience. Only strong emotional attachments have the power to foster heavy hurts, a sense of ill treatment, betrayal even.

Without an ongoing willingness to forgive, two outcomes threaten. One, the connection frays and, while remaining intact, becomes miserable. Two, it unravels. Whoever—spouse, mother, son—walks away or is pushed away.

Your son-in-law has an obnoxious streak, and "I'm about done putting up with him." What then? If you remove him from your sight, does your daughter—his wife—disappear too? Your father smugly takes pot shots at your religion. You've corrected him, but they continue. If you can't ignore them, is your next move to ignore him—completely? When someone is central to your life, forgiveness, too, must be central.

As this book re-repeats, how much another irritates you is more under your control than under his. The less you let that person get to you, the less your temptation to act on the nuclear option: rend the relationship.

There is someone you believe needs your forgiveness, but he doesn't agree. Either he doesn't think he wronged you, or you are the one in the wrong.

After hours of indescribable torture, Jesus prayed from the Cross, "Father, forgive them; for they know not what they do" (Luke 23:34). His tormenters were not only ignorant of their infinite wrongdoing; they reveled in it. Jesus models a lesson in extreme forgiveness. To forgive only those who ask for it puts limits upon whom you forgive.

"She's so sarcastic." "He comes across as if he's special." "He is quick to argue." In short, the behavior is a habit, a pattern. And it gets harder to let pass again and again. Whether sarcasm, arrogance, contrariness—rather than struggling to overlook each instance, overlook the trait.

You have plenty of evidence that this is someone's way, so forgive his way, meaning that particular personality "fault." Trait forgiveness lessens the frustration of "Here we go again." It is a broad blanket that covers repeated "sins."

A man asked me, "Help me be less of a JERK!" (his caps). He told of a close relative he just didn't like. Being around that relative forced the man to be more cordial than he felt (that's good). "He's a good guy, but I just don't relate to him." Furthermore, this relative was unaware of any of this.

When I said the problem sounded like his, he readily agreed. His visceral reaction arose from some vague intolerance, the why of which he hadn't explored, and which he'd best identify and conquer. Otherwise, his "jerkiness" would affect not only him but other family members.

There will always be those with whom we don't mesh well. And neither will they mesh well with us. As long as mistreatment isn't present, neither need forgiveness be.

Psychology 101: Self-interest is a universal motive. Centuries before the modern study of the psyche, St. Thomas Aquinas observed: Follow the self. Reason and emotions routinely yield to self-interest.

To forgive is in one's total self-interest. To overlook, to let go, to pardon slights, to forget wrongs and hurts benefits not only us but our every relationship.

To forgive can be very hard. There is one thing harder: Not to forgive.

Time Limited

The holidays—good-time get-togethers, spirited gabfests, bountiful buffets, connecting with those from six miles or six states distant. A time to gather 'round. Or a time to skip town.

For most, celebrations bring more unity than disunity, more fun than feud. Still, strains can arrive too. Diverse personalities packed close can invite discord.

Uncle Seuss is a grinch. His glass isn't half full; it's two sizes too small. Sunny, your sour cousin, lands in town annually for her Christmas circuit. You're on her schedule, wondering, "Can I yield my time to someone else?" Your mother has a fixed agenda about which of her grown children should visit whom, when, and where. And it's not open to mediation.

Childhood Christmases gave me little stress. Gifts, goodies, and a shuttered school all elevated my mood. Were any adults around me at odds, I didn't notice.

Not that trouble didn't find me. Around my eleventh Christmas, practicing my karate kicks, I capsized our just-ornamented Christmas tree. Dad took the wreckage in stride—the first time around, not so much the second (on the same day).

Toppled trees can't ruin a holiday, but a ruffled relationship can. For one, someone may be present with whom you have little contact 99 percent of the year and would prefer it be 100. Would they prefer the same percentage with you? Just asking.

For another, your contact is concentrated. It is a tight few hours or days around someone who can rankle you in a few minutes.

Whatever the length, it is limited. How long is Christmas dinner? The graduation party? Grandma's birthday bash? You can be sociable, or at least not unsociable, with most anyone for a short enough stretch. Believing so, you'll spend less time fretting about having to be around that person.

Practice time management. Avoid potential arguments. Don't dispute details. Sidestep inflammatory topics. Ignore insensitive remarks—"Have you gained weight?" Should raunchy talk erupt, discreetly slip away. Land somewhere else—the kids' table or the bathroom. How many toilet trips can you make before someone asks, "Are you feeling okay?"

Being likable for a short time with someone you find unlikable is a gift to those you do like. Holidays remind your mother that her eldest son, your estranged brother, swings around home about as often as Halley's comet. She so wants to see all her kids together, if only for a day or so. It makes her feel less like a "failure" as a mother. Alienated siblings spur parental self-doubt. "Where did I go wrong?" is a nagging question.

Upon hearing of your brother's planned stopover, your first thought is "If he's there, I'm not." Can you show up anyway? Is your dislike for your brother stronger than your love for your mother?

"My parents will be here for only a few days. I feel caught between you and them. For my sake, can you make them feel welcome? Please?" A good answer—for your wife, your marriage, her parents, and you—is an unconditional, "I can do that." A good question: "Why is it so hard for me to do something for a short time that would mean so much to my wife?"

Baseball teams have a "closer"—a pitcher who enters the game late to protect a slim lead and "save" the win. They also have a "starter"—a pitcher who opens the game and may be on the mound for several innings. Because he could throw upward of one hundred pitches, he must pace himself. The closer, on the other hand, throws for one, maybe two innings. So he can hurl each pitch with full effort.

In an occasional but still trying relationship, we are like closers. We can exert full energy to get along for a few social innings. We need to persevere just long enough to score a social win.

Almost Everybody?

How to Get Along with Everybody. Why isn't that this book's title? Why the "Almost"? Don't most people want to get along with everybody or, better said, everybody they want to get along with? "Almost" is in the title for this reason: Getting along with everybody is not doable. It's a promise that can't be fulfilled.

That said, most of us will admit we can do better at getting along with others. We can give more compliments, listen longer, be more easygoing, less offendable, quicker to forgive. We can upset ourselves less over their ways and upset them less with ours.

Still, best efforts don't guarantee another will reciprocate. You reach out; they don't reach back. And the reasons may not be all that clear. What is clear is their resistance, marked by few or no return gestures.

Sadly common is the young adult who limits or severs all contact with mother or father, or both. While safety or a chaotic past can be at the root, often neither is. The main motive is dislike: "I don't like the way you raised me." "I don't like your religion." "I don't like your traditional morals." "I don't like your politics." "I don't like you."

Parents are left confused, crushed, and helpless. Roiled by guilt, they scour their family life for hidden failings. "What did we miss? Where did we go wrong?"

Those alienations most painful involve those once warmer—spouse, parent, child, sibling, friend. Histories with misunderstandings and fragile emotions fueled friction ending in fissure.

A grandmother was watching her daughter-in-law withdraw from her, taking her children along. The split being near complete, Grandma admitted, "I know I have my faults. I speak too quickly with too many opinions. But it's not all me. My daughter-in-law can be touchy and hard to please."

"Do you want a good relationship with her?" I asked. Very much. "Is that worth doing whatever you can to try to mend things?" Yes. "Then lay aside your hurts and hard feelings. Apologize for any time you overstepped your bounds. Promise to work hard to no longer do so. Ask to be forgiven." A humbling appeal, one calling for self-surrender but also one with a decent chance for success.

The better apologies are specific: "I was wrong when I said this" or "I regret when I did this." They don't pair with justifications or excuses: "I said that because ..." or "I only did that because you ..."

How much fault is Grandma's and how much is daughter-in-law's is not the issue. Grandma wants relationship rehabilitation, so she may have to assume more blame, even if not all deserved. Pride can successfully undermine any reconciliation.

"How much do I reach out?" Read the cues. How are you being received? A text, voicemail, or card is less personal yet still says, "I'm open to reconnect." How often you reach out depends upon whether you're acknowledged or ignored. Too many tries too fast, even when not overtly spurned, can risk a "Stop. Enough already."

Kenny Rogers's song "The Gambler" antes up this poker-playing tip: "You got to know when to hold 'em, know when to fold 'em, know when to walk away." Sound words for life. Conciliatory actions, apologies, accommodations—all can meet stony silence, if not swelling hostility. Life Rule 101: You can't reach someone if that person doesn't want to be reached. "Leave me alone" forces you to "know when to fold 'em," at least until your hand improves. In the meantime, "hold 'em" with hope: circumstances and maturity can and do change hearts.

Relationships don't always sever from strife. Some just drift apart. Ties are loosened or torn by life's ever-moving currents. Schoolmates, once daily companions, head in different directions with age. Priorities shift, jobs beckon from faraway states, families form. One party still wants to preserve some of what was; the other less so. The friendship doesn't drop from discord, it slips apart. To hold it together takes two.

Social psychologists identify a main shaper of friendships: proximity—physical nearness. People associate naturally with neighbors, co-workers, teammates. They meet in church, school, clubs. When those shared environments shift, so do the shared connections.

Some relationships are outgrown. An e-mail came to me:

> I was pretty fond of the party crowd in college. After graduating, I've grown on fire for my Faith. I still have contact with those "friendships," but I no longer agree with their lifestyle and have a hard time being around them because they still enjoy doing the things we did in college.
>
> Do I stay friends? And how do I do that without compromising what I believe? If I don't stay friends, they could think, "She's now too good for us." And blame my Faith.

The writer is not shunning former friends. She can be friendly without being a friend. How much to associate with her college group is her decision, not theirs. If they refuse to understand, they have, in effect, set the conditions for future contacts.

"I pray always for reconciliation, that someday we will reunite." When counseling those of religious faith, I assume, safely so, that they've been praying for reconciliation. Were I to ask, "Have you prayed about this?" I doubt they'd say, "Thank you. I never thought of that." They've already been sending ardent prayers toward God. For those who believe in a God who listens, prayer can reach across wide emotional divides to move a soul.

It's a rare life completely free of any bruised or broken relationships. It's a far from perfect world with far from perfect people. While not everyone is seemingly moved by prayers, prayers act in unknown and mysterious ways, far beyond our immediate vision. More than forty years as a psychologist has given me plenty of time to watch relationships that looked to be irreconcilable restored.

Personal peace follows from living in the balance between hope and reality.

About the Author

Dr. Ray Guarendi is the father of ten, a clinical psychologist, an author, a public speaker, and a nationally syndicated radio and television host. His radio show, *The Doctor Is In*, can be heard weekdays on EWTN Radio and Sirius/XM satellite radio. Dr. Ray's national television show, *Living Right with Dr. Ray*, is entering its fourteenth season. His many books include *Raising Upright Kids in an Upside-Down World*, *Living Calm*, and *Thinking Like Jesus*.